Flower Arranging for All Occasions

Flower Arranging

for
All Occasions

Revised edition of How to Arrange Flowers for All Occasions

by Katherine Noble Cutler

Illustrations by Rebekah H. Collins

Doubleday & Company, Inc.
Garden City, New York

Revised edition of HOW TO ARRANGE FLOWERS
FOR ALL OCCASIONS by Katherine N. Cutler

Design by Jeanette Portelli

Contents

3 Arrangements for the Home

4 Arrangements for Occasions and Holidays

5 Using Your Talents for Others

Introduction

From earliest civilization man has appreciated and cherished flowers and other plant material. In early Chinese, Japanese, Egyptian, and Greek art, flowers have had an important place. Through the centuries, no dwelling from castle to cottage was without some form of living-plant material. The pioneer women of our country would take precious packets of flower seeds with them on their journeys west, and would grow bright blossoms in utilitarian containers in the windows and around the doorsteps of their crude cabins. These women didn't have time to "arrange" flowers, but they felt a need for them as part of their daily lives.

Flowers are spiritually satisfying. One snowy day recently, a young friend, who had just driven her sister to the airport to board a plane for the Caribbean, said, "I just had to stop on my way home and buy three freesia. I put them on the kitchen table, and every time I look at them I get a lift and forget about this horrible weather and know that spring is coming."

My aim in this book is to try and convey my great enthusiasm and share with you some of the pleasures and problems of many happy flower-arranging years. My hope is that, inspired by the beauty in the world around you, and helped by the knowledge of some fundamental principles of art and mechanical aids, which we will discuss, you will be able to create lovely arrangements and experience the joy that doing so brings.

The next time you are out for a walk, look around you with a "seeing eye" and you may discover something you have not noticed before that could be the nucleus of an interesting arrangement. It might be a beautifully curved pine branch, a gnarled root, early clusters of tree blossoms (yes, many trees have blossoms, often so high that they go unnoticed), an interesting weed, or seedpod. Once you develop this habit you will almost never come home empty-handed.

Some time ago I talked on the subject of this "seeing eye" to school children in Bermuda. As we were riding to the airport in a taxi, on our way back to the states, I said to my husband, "Oh, look at that beautiful curved dried branch by the side of the road." The taxi driver turned around and said, "My kid is always bringing home something like that. Some woman came and talked to the school."

Flower arranging—or as some prefer, "designing with plant material," since this term includes not only flowers but any form of plant material whether living or dried—is a wonderful form of self-expression and can be a truly joyous experience. It should never be approached with trepidation. Too often people are intimidated by experienced arrangers who talk in technical terms used in flower-show schools and classes for exhibitors. The thing to remember is that exhibiting in a flower show and arranging flowers in your home for your own pleasure are two different things. The exhibitor must be knowledgeable in more advanced study to conform to exacting schedules, and this is fine for those whose ambition is in that direction. Admittedly, it is a big thrill to win a blue ribbon in a flower show. However, it is also a thrill to create an arrangement for your own home that pleases you and your guests, even though it might not win any major awards.

I am reminded of one such arrangement I saw the other night. On the mantel were clusters of velvety gray bayberries in a pewter mug. There was neither "line" nor "focal point," but the color and texture were beautifully related, the proportion was good, and the whole effect extremely pleasing. My hostess, who had done it, said, "I can't help saying that I just love it."

As I said before, I hope that inspired by the beauty in the world around you, and helped by the knowledge of some fundamental principles of art and the use of mechanical aids, you will create lovely arrangements. But, above all, I hope you will *enjoy doing it*.

Flower Arranging for All Occasions

1
Basics of Flower Arranging

Principles of Design

People always ask, "What is the first step in making a flower arrangement or designing with plant material? Do you select flowers first and then choose a container for them? Or do you have a favorite container and look for the right flowers to complement it? If a florist arrives with a surprise box of flowers (to me, still one of life's thrilling moments) or a neighbor arrives with an armful of flowers from her garden, do you start by finding the best background for them in your house?" There is no set rule. Any of these methods will work.

Once you have the inspiring element in hand—whether it be the flowers, the container, or the room itself—one of your first thoughts should go to design. Design makes the difference between a distinctive arrangement and one that is dull and will get little notice. And it is often the emphasis placed on design and the technical terms that frightens and bewilders the novice arranger.

Principles of design *are* important but not really difficult to comprehend. You use them instinctively every day in the way you place your furniture, set your table, and choose your clothes. However, a conscious knowledge of these principles and the way they apply to flower arrangements will give you confidence.

Pattern

Each arrangement should have a *pattern* or shape. Often this is suggested by the plant material itself: A curving branch could inspire a crescent shape; snapdragons, which curve in different directions, might inspire a reverse or S curve known as the Hogarth line; or clusters of lilacs might create a lovely round mass arrangement.

Each person has his own way of developing this shape or silhouette. For me it is easiest to make the outline by putting in the main lines first. If my arrangement is circular or crescent-shaped, I establish the main curves. If it is triangular, I put in the vertical piece and then the sidepieces. Once you have established the outline, complete the design by filling in with other material. To make it interesting, try to use different forms—spiky, like stock or larkspur; round, like daisies or carnations; irregular, like daffodils or lilies. To give the arrangement a feeling of dimension, turn some of the flowers in profile, and to give depth, place some toward the back. A flower arrangement has the feeling of a painting and sculpture combined.

Center of Interest

Each arrangement must have what is called a *center of interest*—a place from which the different lines radiate. The center of interest is where the eye comes to rest rather than being aimlessly drawn round and round. As the name suggests, this is usually in the center. This gives the arrangement stability. It is the same principle when you make a fireplace or piano the focal point in a room. Putting larger and darker forms at this center of interest is a common practice.

Balance

It is disconcerting to see an arrangement that looks as though it might tip over at any minute. To avoid this feeling an arrangement must have *balance*. Visual weight is important in flower arranging and is very simple to achieve. I remember giving a talk before a junior flower show to a group of kindergartners. I held up two tulips of identical size, one white and one bright red. I said, "Which of these two flowers is the heaviest?" There was a chorus of "The red one." I explained that it only *looked* heavier because of the dark color, but that if the two were put on a scale they would weigh about the same. Then I said, "Since the red tulip looks heavier, let's pretend it is a boy in the sixth grade and the white one is a boy from your class. If one of you were on a seesaw with a boy from the sixth grade, where would he have to sit to make the seesaw balance?" Again there was a chorus of "Near the middle." I explained then that for a flower arrangement to be properly balanced, the larger and darker flowers should be toward the middle and the smaller and lighter flowers nearer the edge. The children got the point so well that on the day of the show there was a big red flower in the middle of almost every kindergartner's arrangement!

Sometimes it happens that in the material you are using the darkest color is in the smallest flowers, like violets or purple sweet peas. You might say to yourself, "What do I do now? They say the small flowers belong toward the outside of an arrangement and the dark ones toward the middle. How can these be both places?" The solution is easy. Group the small dark flowers into a bunch and use them as you would one flower, near the center.

Proportion

There must be good *proportion* in a flower arrangement. The general suggestion for achieving this is that the plant material should be one and a half times the height of a tall container, or one and a half times the width of a low one. This is not a rule—merely a guide. An arrangement can be much taller than one and a half times the size of a tall vase if there is great visual weight in the container. For instance, if you were using white mock orange in a tall bronze container, the sprays of mock orange could be three times as tall as the vase because the great visual weight of the tall heavy bronze container can support unusually tall branches of the small white flowers. If you are in doubt, you would be safe to stick with the one-and-a-half-times rule, but don't take it too literally; experiment and use your creative senses.

Rhythm

Your design should have *rhythm*. This is accomplished by the repetition of form and color that makes the lines of the arrangement flow into each other and leads the eye from the center of interest through the arrangement and back to it again. Solid forms decrease in size from the center, and spaces or voids increase.

Suitability

There should be *suitability* in the relationship between the material and the container of an arrangement. This is almost self-explanatory. Just as a woman would not wear sport shoes with an evening dress, I don't think she would put fragile lilies or orchids in a coarse pottery bowl or dandelions in a silver container. There should be a relationship between the flowers and container in both quality and texture. Suitability does not necessarily mean whether a flower is expensive to buy. For instance, roadside daisies would look perfect in a silver container because of their dainty form and satiny texture.

Scale

Scale is important, too. Again it is a principle that most people use instinctively. Just as you would not fill a small living room with heavy Empire furniture or offer a child's chair to an adult to sit on, you should not use a five-inch-tall vase for heavy flowers like dahlias. Think of the size of the flowers and choose a container that gives them visual support so that the flowers do not overpower it, or it overpower the flowers.

Color

Color is one of the most important elements to be considered when designing an arrangement. The following section is devoted to this subject.

Texture

There should be a strong relationship of *texture* between flowers and container. When you look at them you can sense a tactile quality. You don't have to actually touch a pansy to know that it feels smooth and velvety. Looking at a pewter container with a smooth patina gives you much the same feeling. Therefore you can be sure that pansies arranged in a pewter container would be a happy combination. Zinnias and strawflowers have a rough look, as do weathered wood, wicker, and driftwood. There would be a kinship there.

These are safe combinations, but it does not mean that you have to use flowers and containers of the same textural feeling. Often the introduction of a *contrast* makes the arrangement more interesting. Be aware of the textural qualities of your materials and use them with thought for the best effect.

Form

There are three basic types of design—line arrangements, line mass arrangements, and mass arrangements.

A line arrangement is composed of linear plant material such as a bare branch, a curved leaf like aspidistra or sansevieria, or the curves of a vine like wisteria. The linear material is dominant and spaces are used to emphasize this.

A line mass arrangement is a line arrangement to which more plant material has been added to support the original line without obscuring its design. In other words, line is still dominant but other materials are used to complement it.

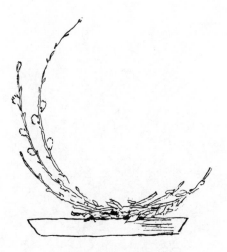

Line Arrangement

Line Mass Arrangement

A mass arrangement is a solid mass of flowers, as in a bouquet, with less spaces than in the other two. Period arrangements—those that have been associated with different periods of civilization such as Renaissance, Baroque, Georgian, Victorian, and Early American—are usually mass arrangements.

In designing a flower arrangement, a form or shape should be kept in mind. The arrangement might take the shape of a triangle, a crescent, an oval, a circle, an S curve, a vertical, a horizontal, or any other rec-

Round Mass Arrangement

ognizable shape. However, whatever the shape, the arrangement will still be either a line, a line mass, or a mass arrangement. Let me illustrate: You could make a crescent-shaped arrangement with wands of pussy willow. This would be a *line arrangement* with a *crescent shape.* If you added some tulips, following but not obscuring the line of the pussy willows, it would still be a crescent shape but would be a *line mass arrangement.*

You can make a *mass arrangement* in a *round shape,* but a mass arrangement could also have a *triangular shape.*

Triangle Mass Arrangement

An arrangement may be symmetrical or asymmetrical. If symmetrical, the outline of the arrangement is the same on either side of an imaginary vertical axis. In an asymmetrical arrangement, the outline is not the same on either side of the axis, but the visual balance must be.

The principles discussed in this chapter apply to what's known as traditional arrangements—those that have stood the test of years and are the ones that fit into most people's lives.

Today an interest in creativity and in new trends has emerged and has led to new developments in flower arranging—we will touch on

Symmetrical Arrangement

these in later sections—but traditional arrangements will always be with us.

When you complete an arrangement give yourself this little test. Ask:

1. Is there a definite pattern in the arrangement?
2. Does it have a dimensional look?
3. Are there different flower forms?
4. Is there a center of interest?

5. Is the color harmonious and carried through the arrangement?
6. Is the plant material high or wide enough for the size of the container?
7. Is the material related to the container in scale?
8. Have I been conscious of textural qualities?
9. Are the flowers and container suitable in quality?
10. Do I like this arrangement?
11. Have I enjoyed making it?

If you can answer "yes" to the first ten questions, you can be confident that you have made a good arrangement and that it will please others too. If you can answer "yes" to the last question, you have found a means of self-expression that will bring you joy and inspiration for the rest of your life.

Assymetrical Arrangement

Color

Color is one of the most fascinating aspects of designing with plant material. Not only does the balancing of light and dark tones contribute to design, but color is a definite form of communication. Cool colors like green and blue give a feeling of serenity; a brilliant contrast of strong colors is exciting; a blending of soft colors is peaceful; and certain dull ones are definitely depressing.

Flower arrangers should have a basic knowledge of color theory. However, since you are working with colors that already exist, the approach is different than that of a painter who can mix his own. The whole subject of color is so complex—entire books are written about it —but it is not necessary for the flower arranger to go deeply into the academic and scientific sides of the subject. It *is* important, however, to understand the *relationship* between colors in order to develop a color sense, and to learn color terminology in order to understand and discuss it.

A way to learn about color relationship, which is fun and instructive, is to make a color wheel or circle. To do so:

1. Draw a circle and divide it into twelve segments as though you were cutting a pie and, as an added aid, number the segments.
2. Place the names of the three primary colors (so called because they cannot be produced by mixing any colors together) equidistantly around the circle, starting with Yellow in segment 1. Red would then be in 5 and Blue in 9.
3. Mixing equal parts of Yellow and Red produces Orange, so put it equidistant between its parents or segment 3.
4. In the same way, mixing Red and Blue produces Violet, and Blue and Yellow, Green. Therefore, put these two new colors between their parents, Violet in segment 7 and Green in 11.
5. Now we come to a third set of colors, made by mixing the colors either side of the empty segments, which will make Yellow-

Orange in segment 2, Red-Orange in 4, Red-Violet in 6, Blue-Violet in 8, Blue-Green in 10, and Yellow-Green in 12.

You will see that half of the circle, from Yellow to Red-Violet is made up of strong colors and the other half from Violet to Yellow-Green of cool colors.

Although white, black, and gray are sometimes called colors, they are really neutrals since black is the absence of color and white is the presence of all colors. Black, white, and gray are used to form gradations of the twelve parent colors shown on the color wheel.

It is useful to know color terminology.

Hue: This is the common name given to the twelve colors on the wheel. It is the parent color.

Tint: This is the color produced by adding white to a hue. Thus pink is a tint of red.

Shade: This is the color produced by adding black to the parent hue. Thus brown is a shade of yellow. (I remember the difference between tint and shade by thinking that pulling down a window shade makes things darker.)

Tone: This is a hue mixed with gray, but it is also used for all colors that deviate from a pure hue. Thus you might hear someone, admiring an arrangement in various colors of green, refer to it as "shades of green." This would be incorrect. The correct statement would be "tones of green" as this includes both tints and shades.

Although there are names for different color schemes, the enjoyment of working with colors in flower arrangements is to experiment, following your own taste and color sense. However, as a guide, we will mention three of the best known:

Complementary Color Scheme: This is a color scheme using colors that are exactly opposite on the color wheel. It is safe and satisfying because it balances strong and cool colors. We often see it in nature, as in the bright red berries and green leaves of holly.

Monochromatic Color Scheme: This is a color scheme as its name suggests, mono (single) chroma (color), of tints and shades of a single hue. This might range in tints and shades of yellow from palest cream to dark brown.

Analogous Color Scheme: This is using colors that are adjacent to each other on the color wheel. For instance, an arrangement of pink roses, rose carnations, red-violet sweet peas, lavender stock, and purple petunias would be an analogous color scheme.

Choice of color is a very personal thing. There are certain colors that you may prefer to others. You use them in your home or your clothes, and you will probably use them in your flower arrangements too. This feeling of personal color preference is so strong that one of the important instructions given to student judges at flower school judging courses is that they must never be influenced in a decision by personal color preference.

Color is a very important element in the design of a flower arrangement. Dark colors have greater visual *weight*. Therefore if flowers with darker colors are not placed strategically in a design, they destroy the balance. The youngster knows that, in order to make a seesaw balance properly, the heavier of two children must sit toward the middle. So, given two flowers of the same size but one darker than the other, the darker flower, because of its visual weight, must be placed toward the center.

To be effective, color should not be spotted through the design but should be placed so that there is *transition* from one to the other. A common mistake of the novice arranger is to concentrate color either at the top or bottom of a design so that the arrangement appears to be cut in half. For instance, because daffodils are larger and stronger in color than daisies, you might put all the daffodils near the bottom and center and all the daisies near the top. This would make the arrangement look cut in half. To correct this, a few of the daisies should be placed among the daffodils and some daffodil buds near the top with the daisies.

Rhythm in a flower arrangement can be established with the color of the flowers. If there is a transition of color from the center of interest in the middle to the outside edges—for example, from deep red roses through deep pink roses to pale pink at the top and sides—your eye moves rhythmically through the arrangement.

Strong colors advance visually, and cool colors recede. This is important to remember, particularly in a very large room or a church. Someone who is not aware of this might make an arrangement on a church altar, using flowers like blue delphinium or purple iris in a mass arrangement. From the rear of the church, the arrangement would seem to have blank spaces in them as the cool colors do not carry but a short distance.

On the other hand, certain colors have radiant qualities, seeming to shed light, particularly yellow, orange, and yellow-green. Many expert arrangers make a point of using some yellow-green, chartreuse, or lime-green foliage in their arrangements for this reason. White, although not technically a color, has great luminosity and tends to compete rather than blend with strong colors. White is more pleasing when it is combined with tints rather than hues.

It is exciting when assembling an arrangement to discover unexpected *color accents*—to see, for instance, how the dark red underside of a begonia leaf will pick up a pink highlight in a bronze container, or how the petals of a hydrangea will have a green cast when placed against a celadon-green wall. You can use color in a flower arrangement to emphasize another color in a room. I realized this one day in the fall when I went out to see what I could find to make an arrangement in the living room. There were no flowers but plenty of foliage, so I gathered laurel, deep green ilex, chartreuse andromeda, and, for a center of interest, some dogwood leaves that were a gorgeous deep red. When I put the arrangement on a table, the same red of the dogwood leaves sprang at me from various places in the room—a subordinate color note in the draperies, some tiny flowers on a needlepoint chair, some books in the bookshelves, and a red enamel ashtray on a coffee table. The dogwood leaves drew them all together.

Effect of Lighting on Arrangement

Whenever possible you should do an arrangement in the place you have chosen for it, as light has a definite effect on the design and color. Strong light from one source—like a nearby window—will cause deeper shadows, giving greater depth to the design.

Fluorescent lighting tends to give reds an unattractive brown color, but intensifies blue tones. Good daylight brings out the best in the cool colors of blue and violet. In weak lighting, such as candlelight, many colors seem to disappear, but it is safe to use bright and shiny colors with high luminosity.

Glossy table surfaces reflect light and will emphasize highlights in the arrangement.

Selecting and Conditioning Plant Material

The more you train yourself to have a "seeing eye," the easier it will be for you to find interesting and unusual plant material. It is amazing how, once your eye becomes trained, you can't walk through a garden, in the woods and fields, or along the roadside without seeing things you might never have noticed before. If you see a branch that intrigues you, discipline yourself to look at the skeletal line without being confused by leaves and side branches. Notice how these can be trimmed away to emphasize the main line.

In choosing flowers, notice their variety of shapes. The most successful arrangement combines a variety of forms. Daisies, carnations, and zinnias are round; delphinium, lupines, stock, snapdragons, and foxgloves are spiky; fuchsia and wisteria are pendulant; daffodils and columbine are irregular. (See chart at the end of this section for Plant Material According to Shape.)

There is the same variety of form in leaves. Geranium and galax leaves are round; iris and sansevieria are spiky; tradescantia and philodendron are pendulant; and rex begonia and ivy are irregular. When you are making an arrangement and want a certain form that your flowers don't have, try substituting foliage in the desired shape.

When you buy flowers at a florist's, try to get a few buds. Some flowers, like spray carnations or spray chrysanthemums, pinks and marguerites, have them attached to the main stem. Buying a few buds will be worth the cost in added interest to an arrangement.

Making Your Arrangement Last

The length of time that an arrangement will last depends greatly on the manner in which the material is conditioned. This is very important because an arrangement with properly conditioned material will last days longer than one that has had little preparation.

The Key
Is Cutting

The first step in conditioning is cutting: Cut flowers in the morning or late afternoon, if possible, so that the midday sun won't wilt them. Make a slanting cut with a sharp knife so that there will be more surface to absorb water. A knife is better than shears because if the shears are at all dull the stems will be torn or crushed, inhibiting the intake of water.

Carry a container of water with you so that as you gather flowers you can put them in water immediately. You can make a convenient carrier for this purpose by taking three different-sized fruit-juice cans to a tinsmith and having him solder them together around a tall rod for carrying. You can arrange them in this container according to stem size as you gather them.

Strip off any foliage that would be submerged, especially that of marigolds and chrysanthemums. If you don't, the foliage will decay and will foul the water and weaken the stems.

Strip foliage and thorns from roses by holding the flowers in one hand and stripping off the leaves and thorns with a wad of newspaper held in the other hand. Removing the thorns opens more water-absorbing areas.

Remove pollen from lilies and tulips to make them last longer.

Recut the stems of florist flowers and leave the flowers in deep water for several hours or overnight.

Bulbs, such as tulips, narcissus, and hyacinths, may have beady drops of moisture on the ends of the stems when you cut them. Wipe this moisture away. Otherwise it will seal the ends of the stems and prevent water from entering.

Hardening—
Submerging Your
Flowers in Water

Some decorative foliage does wilt quickly, but if you submerge it in water, preferably overnight, it will last for days. Do this for calla lily leaves, Japanese maple, ivy leaves, begonia leaves, and the new growth of roses and peonies. Violets will keep best if you completely immerse them for a while.

Camellias, gardenias, and orchids do not need to be in water after they are cut, but they keep best when surrounded with moisture. Sprinkle them lightly, then put them on a bed of moist tissue in a box and keep them in a cool place.

Some plants require special treatment before being put in water to soak, or *harden,* as it is called. The reasons for this are simple: Some flowers have a milky juice in the stems. If this juice drips away, the cells collapse and the flowers will droop. To prevent the juice from escaping, sear the end of the cut immediately. You might take a candle and some matches with you for this purpose, or a cigarette lighter. Flowers that need this treatment are milkweed, dahlias, pokeweed, poinsettias, mignonette, heliotrope, poppies, hollyhocks, and morning glories. In the case of shrubs with very heavy stems like lilacs, it helps to crush the ends of the stems with a heavy object.

It may be a good idea to say a special word about lilacs because it seems to me that more questions are asked about hardening this shrub than any other. This is the way I have had the most success:

Three Ways to Condition Plant Material

If flowers exude milky juice, sear stem ends.

Strip thorns from rose stems with wad of paper.

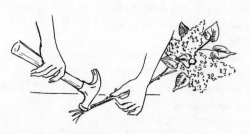

Crush stem ends of woody shrubs.

First I strip off the leaves on the stems, leaving just one cluster near the flower head to help conduct water to it. Then I slit the stems about three inches and bang a hammer on the ends a few times, to increase the water-absorbing area. Then I put them in deep water overnight. After this treatment they usually last beautifully.

It is not necessary to harden evergreens. Rhododendrons, however, will be more graceful in an arrangement after several days hardening to let the leaves relax. Some people use oils or other preparations to shine the leaves of broad-leaved evergreens, but you can give them a very natural-looking shine by cleaning them with warm soapy water and then rubbing them to a gloss with waxed paper.

There are many theories about various formulas to put into water to make flowers last longer. Whether or not they really do any good is a debatable question, but they don't do any harm. If someone passes a pet theory on to you, go ahead and experiment. The chances are, though, that if your flowers are fresh and are put in fresh water, they will last the maximum amount of time anyway.

Well-hardened flowers should last as well in a shallow bowl as in a deep one, providing you keep topping with water to compensate for evaporation. It isn't necessary to recut stems or completely change the water—in fact it is better not to do so, as the more flowers are handled, the quicker they will wilt.

Place completed arrangements where they will be out of direct drafts and away from coal and gas fumes or the heat of a fireplace. All of these things will shorten the life of plant material.

Using
Hot Water

It is only recently that I have learned a phase of conditioning material that continues to amaze and delight me. This is the use of *very* hot, practically boiling water. It has been our good fortune to have as a houseguest, on his recent trips to the United States, an internationally known flower arranger from England. It is from him that I have learned the restorative effect of hot water on plant material. He would come back from a demonstration with dogwood, roses, calla lilies, and other flowers so wilted that they seemed destined for the trash bin. Not so! In they went, after recutting the stems, into deep, extremely hot water, the heads of the flowers either hanging over the edge of the container or protected by tissue or plastic, and miraculously the flowers revived to the point where they were available for the next day's demonstration. A few did not make it, of course, but most did.

Last year, on a trip around the world by ship, I was scheduled to give a flower-arranging demonstration on board. On shore, in Malaysia, I was driving around looking for material when I spied something pink growing in a ditch of fern on the edge of a rubber plantation. On investigation, I found to my delight that it was wild pink caladium— exquisite miniatures of the large greenhouse plants to which I was accustomed. I gathered a bunch of them. By the time we got back to the ship they were completely limp and wilted. Previously I would have regretfully thrown them away, but with my new knowledge of the hot-water treatment, I filled the washbasin with very hot water and put the caladium in it. In a comparatively short time they had completely revived and remained sturdy and beautiful for my demonstration two days later.

Flowers That Condition Well with Hot Water

Bleeding heart	Hydrangeas
Clematis	Jasmine
Dahlias	Mock Orange
Honeysuckle	Wisteria

1. First, put flowers (with the heads hanging out) for ten to fifteen seconds in about two inches of very hot water in the bottom of a container.

2. Then fill the container with cool water.

3. Let the flowers remain in cool water for several hours.

**Shaping
Your
Flowers**

There are ways to change the shape of flower stems as they are hardening. Tulips, for instance, are one of the most beautiful, but admittedly one of the most difficult, flowers to arrange. If you want the stems to curve, they stubbornly stand up straight; if you want them straight, they often curve. You can manage them successfully if you pick them in tight bud and wrap the ones you want to be straight in a tube of newspaper, fastening it tightly around the stems up to the heads of the flowers with elastic bands. Soak them that way overnight in a tall container. Let the ones you want to curve hang over the side of the container.

If spiky flowers like snapdragon and stock are stiff and you want them to curve, soak them in a pail with the tips hanging over the edge. They curve beautifully as they try to assume their vertical position.

Training tulips to stand straight or to curve

Helping straight stalks to curve

To make stiff material like palm boots, palm spathes, corn husks and dried vines like wisteria supple, soak in very hot water. You can create intriguing shapes. Roots and heavy branches can actually be boiled to make them manageable. In fact it is great fun to experiment. If there is something you want to shape, try boiling it. You can clean weathered wood with a stiff brush after boiling. If you want a bleached effect on wood, scrub it with a strong solution of laundry bleach.

**Dry
Storage**

Try dry storage if you want to keep flowers for future arrangements; you can pick them at the right time of their bloom and use them for a forthcoming show. Dry flowers with a paper towel so that they are free of moisture, and put them in a plastic bag in the refrigerator. When you are ready to use them, recut the stems and leave them in deep water overnight. Flowers will usually keep about a week and possibly longer.

Helpful Hints for Conditioning Plant Material

1. Strip thorns from rose stems. This provides greater area for water.
2. Crush the ends of stems of woody shrubs such as lilac with a hammer.
3. If flowers wilt before time, recut stems under water as there may be a bubble of air preventing passage of water.
4. Remove pollen from lilies.
5. Immerse violets in water.
6. If a bead of moisture forms on bottom of hollow-stem flowers such as tulips, cut stem above it and immediately put in water.
7. Submerge decorative foliage leaves like calla, Japanese maple, ivy, new growth of roses and peonies.
8. Place the following in two inches of very hot water for ten to fifteen seconds and then fill container with cool water:
   Bleeding Heart
   Clematis
   Dahlias
   Honeysuckle
   Hydrangeas
   Jasmine
   Mock Orange
   Wisteria
9. Air plants, or "floppers," do not need to be in water. They last well in damp sand.
10. To make stiff material such as palm spathes, corn husks, and dried vines supple, soak in very hot water.
11. Wrap tulips for the length of the stem in a tube of newspaper and stand in water overnight to keep stems straight.
12. Keep gardenias and camellias in airtight bag until ready to use.
13. If flowers like poppies or euphorbia have milky sap, char the stems with a match or cigarette lighter to seal stems and keep sap from draining out.

Plant Material According to Shape

Round Flowers	*Spiky Flowers*	*Pendulant Flowers*	*Irregular Flowers*
African Daisy	Artemisia	Acacia	Ageratum
Anemone	Astilbe	Billbergia	Amaryllis
Aster	Bridal Wreath	Bittersweet	Calla
Azalea	Broom	Bleeding Heart	Canna
Bachelor's Button	Campanula	Bougainvillea	Columbine
Begonia	Delphinium	Cup-and-Saucer	Coralbell
(Tuberous)	Flowering	Fuchsia	Daffodil
Calendula	branches	Golden Chain	Day Lily
California Poppy	Forsythia	Tree	Easter Lily
Camellia	Foxglove	Grapes	Forget-me-not
Candytuft	Gladiolus	Honeysuckle	Freesia
Carnation	Goldenrod	Jasmine	Fritillaria
Christmas Rose	Heather	Lantana	Grape Hyacinth
Chrysanthemum	Hyacinth	Orchid	Gypsophila
Cineraria	Larkspur	Pepper Berry	Iris
Clarkia	Liatris	Smilax	Lily of the Valley
Clematis	Lilac	Snowberry	Meadow Rue
Cockscomb	Lupine	Trumpet Vine	Narcissus
Cosmos	Mock Orange	Wisteria	Petunia
Crape Myrtle	Monkshood		Plumbago
Dahlia	Penstemon	*Pendulant*	Primula
Daisy	Physostegia	*Foliage*	Rubrum Lily
Dogwood	Poker Plant		Sweet Pea
Gaillardia	Salvia	Clematis	Tuberose
Geranium	Stock	Grape Ivy	Tulip
Godetia	Tamarix	Ivy	Viola
Hibiscus	Thermopsis	Jade Plant	Violet
Hydrangea	Wallflower	Pothos	
Magnolia	Weigelia	Smilax	*Irregular Foliage*
Marguerite	Yucca	Tradescantia	
Marigold			Begonia (Angel
Pansy	*Spiky Foliage*		Wing)
Passionflower			Begonia (Rex)
Peony	Aspidistra		Caladium
Poinsettia	Canna		Coleus
Poppy	Croton		Maple
Ranunculus	Dracaena		Philodendron
Rose	Iris		
Scabiosa	Narcissus		
Sweet William	Pandanus		
Tulip Tree	Sansevieria		
Flower			
Zinnia			

Round Foliage

Begonia
  (Beefsteak)
Galax
Geranium
Hosta
Sea Grape

Mechanical Aids

One of the most frustrating aspects of making a flower arrangement is when you have a mental picture of how you want it to look but are unable to make the flowers stay in the position you want them. Fortunately, there are many mechanical aids available to make it much easier for arrangers to achieve the designs they have in mind. Just as a cook has his or her favorite tools and a seamstress hers, a flower arranger needs a supply of aids. Only someone who has worked with makeshift mechanics can appreciate the supplies that have come on the market in recent years. If you collect some of these and keep them handy in a drawer or garden basket, many of your arranging problems will be solved.

Knife or Shears

It is best to have two pairs of shears, one for cutting flowers, and another for cutting heavy stems and wire. A small sharp knife is excellent for cutting stems as it makes a clean cut without "chewing" the ends. *Always* cut on the slant. For flowers I prefer the Japanese kind with large oval handles and short sharp blades sometimes known as "butterfly" shears. Keep them sharp because a ragged cut from dull shears seals the stem of a flower and keeps it from absorbing water. After years of exasperation in losing my shears underneath material as I worked, I have learned to paint the handles a bright red.

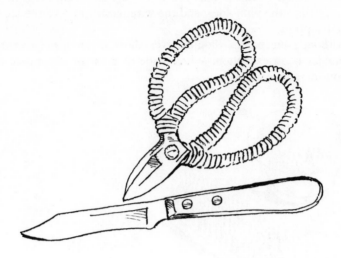

"Butterfly" shears and small paring knife

Pinholders

A pinholder is a device to hold flowers upright in a container. These are made in many shapes and sizes and consist of a heavy metal base with sharp pins, placed close together, protruding from it. You can impale a stem firmly on the pins and lean it to any desired angle. A tall vase may be filled three quarters with sand with a pinholder placed on top so that flowers may be used whose stems are not long enough to reach to the bottom of the vase. It doesn't pay to buy a cheap pinholder as the space between the individual pins is too wide to be efficient, and the pins themselves are weak and soon bend under the weight of any but the lightest stems.

Pinholders are also made encased in a metal cup which will hold water. You can use these on a flat plate, a board, driftwood, or any container you can't fill with water. Because of the weight of the metal cup, these are useful for holding heavy branches. You can make a cup pinholder yourself by fastening a regular pinholder in a flat can like a tuna-fish can with florists' clay or candle wax.

You can also get a pinholder that has a cage of heavy metal over it. The advantage of this is that you can insert stems through the holes in the cage into the pinholder, and the wire mesh will give the stems additional support.

Although mechanics should never show in an arrangement, a cup pinholder is an exception. When made of brass or decorative metal, it is considered a container.

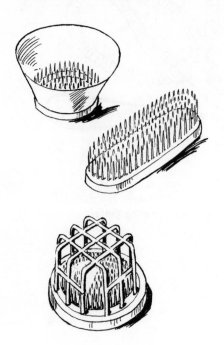

Pinholders

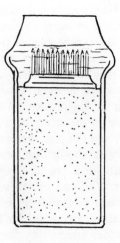

Pinholder on sand

As an emergency substitute for a pinholder, a tall container packed with vertical pieces of plant material such as privet or fern, sheared across the top, will hold flowers upright so that they don't fall to the sides.

Oasis

In recent years a boon to arrangers has come on the market in a material called Oasis. Oasis is a block of porous material. It is feather light when dry and heavy when soaked. At one time it was necessary to soak it for a couple of hours, and this type is still available, but there is a newer variety called Instant Oasis. It will be saturated if you hold it under running water for a minute or two or immerse it in a pail or bowl. Flowers can be inserted in Oasis at any angle, and they will stay fresh. No other water is needed in the container.

Oasis is wonderful for use in a low widemouthed container like a Revere bowl or a soup tureen. Be sure to use a piece large enough to wedge against the sides of the container so it won't slip. For a very firm foundation for a large mass arrangement, anchor a pinholder to the bottom of the container with florists' clay or Stickum and press the block of Oasis on it. The only problem is that bits of Oasis become wedged between the pins of the pinholder and are a nuisance to remove. You can solve this by putting a piece of nylon stocking over the pinholder before you impale the Oasis. Then when you remove the Oasis from the pinholder, the bits that are wedged come out with the piece of nylon when you remove it.

You can insert flower stems into Oasis at any angle. If you want some of the material to hang over the edge of the container, use a block of Oasis large enough to extend above the mouth of the container. Then you can stick the flower stems up into it. You can use a block of Oasis more than once. Put it on a newspaper to dry then store it until you need it again. When it is finally too full of holes to use as a block, crumble it and use it to stuff a tall vase.

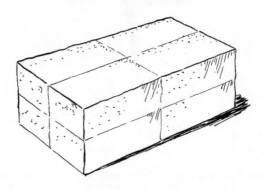

A block of Oasis

Metal Oasis holder

There are now available small round metal saucers with a metal frame in the middle and round plugs of Oasis that just fit into the frame. These are useful for small bouquets, centerpieces for small tables, or for using at intervals on long tables.

Oasis is not to be confused with *Styrofoam,* which also comes in a lightweight block of porous material but which does not hold water and is used with dried material. All of these aids are sold at a florist's.

Picks

Picks—either the short pieces of wood with a thin wire extending from the top that you buy at a florist's, or the thin ones sold for cocktail olives or cherries, or even wooden toothpicks—are a great help to the arranger. For instance, if you are making a spring arrangement and want a group of violets at the base, pinholders will not support the thin

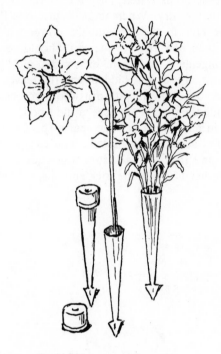

Orchid in water pick

stems. However, if you bunch some of the flowers together, holding them against a florist's pick and winding the wire firmly around the stems, you can then insert the pick into a pinholder, hiding it behind the flowers. Or perhaps you are using carnations and the relatively weak stem bends with the weight of the large blossom. Wire a pick to the carnation stem and stick them both in a pinholder. The pick will help support the stem so that it will stand upright.

Cocktail picks and *toothpicks* are especially useful in fruit arrangements. Fruits piled on top of one another will not roll off if the end of a pick in one piece of fruit is thrust into the piece of fruit beneath it. A bunch of grapes wired at the stem to a florist's pick can hang gracefully over the edge of a compote or bowl if the pick is inserted into a piece of fruit above it.

In the past, when making wreaths and swags, it was customary to wire each piece of material into the background individually. You can now wire cones, fruit, ribbons, and other component parts to picks and stick them into the greens or Styrofoam you are using as a base.

Another type of pick is called an *orchid* or *water pick*. These are small plastic tubes that taper to a pointed wedge, and come with a removable rubber cap with a hole in the middle. The water pick, as the name suggests, holds water. They are useful to hold small flowers in a pinholder that is dry. When there is just one flower, you can put it through the hole in the cap and the flower will stay in place. If you have more than one, remove the cap. Should you want some greens in a fruit arrangement, put them in a water pick, put the pick between pieces of fruit so that it is hidden, and the leaves will stay fresh. If you want to use some flowers with driftwood, you can put them in a water pick and hide the pick in crevices in the wood.

Perhaps in making an arrangement a special tall stem that you need for the top is accidentally broken. You can put the broken piece in a water pick and tape the pick to a firm stick long enough to make up the required height. Hide the stick and pick behind other flowers.

Picks used to hold fruit together and to fasten bunches of grapes so that they will fall gracefully.

Florists' Clay

Sometimes pinholders will slip if they are not fastened to the container. One way to fasten them is with a substance called florists' clay. This comes in a small roll and you can buy it at a florist shop. Soften it by molding it in your hands. It can be used over and over again.

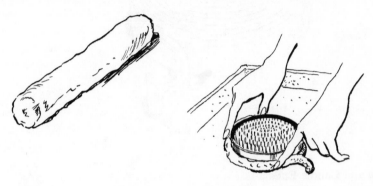

To fasten a pinholder to the bottom of a container, roll a piece of clay between the palms of your hands until it makes a "worm." Then, making sure that both container and pinholder are absolutely dry, press the roll of clay around the edge of the pinholder so that it seals it to the container.

Florists' clay has many other uses—plugging a small hole in a container, filling in an uneven place in a container so that a pinholder won't tip, or mending a broken stem.

Note: Florists' clay will tarnish silver; so if you are using a silver container, use paraffin as described in this chapter.

Stickum

I like to use Stickum because it is absolutely adhesive. However, it is more expensive than florists' clay. Stickum is flattened into a strip about a half inch wide, backed by paper, and formed into a large roll like a roll of tape. You can unwind as much as you need, strip off the paper, and use it as you would clay. It seems absolutely slipproof and anything fastened with it stays in place as though it were glued. You can remove all traces of it with gasoline, naphtha, or nail-polish remover.

It is useful for fastening pieces of driftwood together, fastening water picks to driftwood, plugging holes, fastening candles in holders, and much more (including fastening on my husband's false moustache one Halloween). As with clay, make sure that the things you are fastening together are perfectly dry. Stickum is available at florist shops.

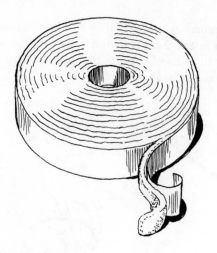

Paraffin and Candle Ends

When you want to fasten a pinholder in a silver or pewter container, you can use paraffin instead of clay which stains. I always keep a few candle ends in my flower-arranging drawer for this purpose. Melt the candles (or a block of paraffin) in a pan and let it cool until it is slightly thickened. Make sure that both pinholder and container are dry. Then put the pinholder in place and pour the wax over the edge of the pinholder where it joins the container.

Some of the most elegant containers are made of alabaster. Many an unhappy arranger has found that alabaster disintegrates on contact with water. If you are fortunate enough to have an alabaster epergne or compote, you can protect it by pouring some melted paraffin in it and gently turning it until all surfaces that will come in contact with water are covered.

Another handy use for paraffin is to put a few drops in the center of a water lily to keep it from closing. You can make a passionflower stay open to float in a bowl or to wear, by dipping it quickly facedown in melted paraffin. Be sure that the temperature is tepid. Immediately after dipping it into the paraffin, dip it into a bowl of ice water to harden the wax.

Pill Bottles

By all means save clear glass or plastic tubular pill bottles for aids. You can use them like water picks for small flowers in your design if you are not using a pinholder. The flat bottoms will rest on a flat surface where the wedge of a water pick will not. You can also fasten them like water picks to sticks, to compensate for broken stems or to place flowers higher in an arrangement. They will also hold large leaves with short stems like angel wing or rex begonia at the focal point of an arrangement. One of the more fascinating ways to use pill bottles is in making a dish garden with flowers, a description of which is given on page 152.

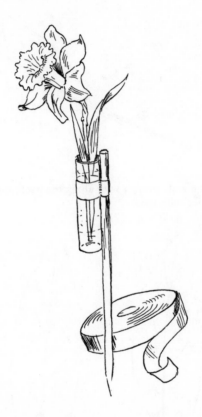

Wire

Wire is at times indispensable in making a flower arrangement. It is sold in different thicknesses called gauges. The gauges range from 18, the strongest, to 26, the finest. Fine wire is used to fasten into bunches small flowers like lilies of the valley, violets, or sweet peas to use as clusters. Use heavier wire when making bunches of greens for wreaths, garlands, or swags. Pieces of the heavier wire are also used as false stems for dried flowers.

If you want pussy willow, Scotch broom, podocarpus, or similar material to curve in certain directions, you can bend them into the desired shape, fasten wire around the bends to hold them in position, and leave them overnight in water. When you remove the wire, the material will usually stay in the form you have bent it.

If a large leaf that you want to use is limp, you can make it stay upright by carefully threading a piece of thin wire up the main vein at the back of the leaf.

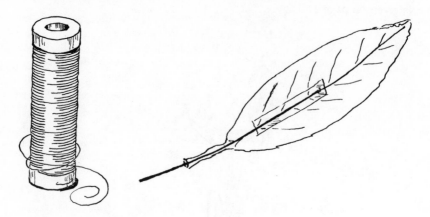

To strengthen a leaf: place a wire along the back middle rib and fasten it in place with tape.

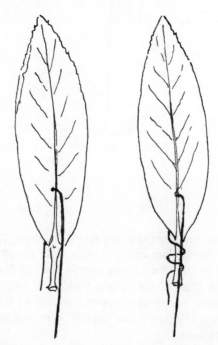

To provide a longer stem for a leaf: thread wire through the base of the leaf, bend the end down and wire the two ends together.

Chicken Wire

Chicken wire, sometimes called wire netting, is a wire mesh readily obtainable at a hardware store. It is especially useful for filling containers where Oasis is not used. For this use, the best is a 2-inch mesh of 18-gauge wire. A smaller mesh when crumpled doesn't leave large enough holes for stems to slide through. Cut a piece as wide as the container and three to four times its depth. Then crumple it, and cram it into the container with the cut ends up. (These can be bent around the rim of the container if desired.) The holes in the crumpled wire will hold stems quite successfully, and the cut edges are great for holding stems in position by bending them around the stems.

A piece of wire mesh can be cut a little larger than the mouth of a container in which Oasis is used, and bent over the rim to hold Oasis in place. Wire netting is not appropriate for a flat container as it is too hard to conceal.

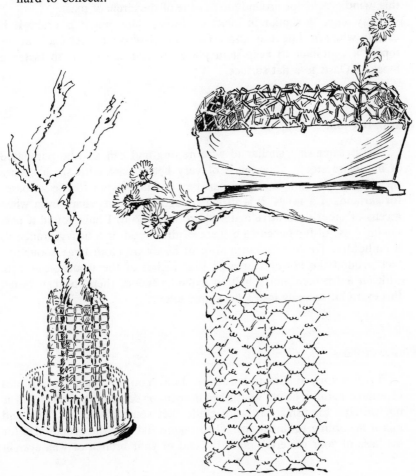

Tape

Flower arrangers use several kinds of tape. One of the most useful is *Scotch Tape*. Probably most of us remember putting the stem of a dandelion in our mouths, when we were children, to watch it curl. It isn't as much fun when you are making an arrangement of daffodils or narcissus and notice that the stems are curled in that same way. A piece of Scotch Tape fastened around the stem ends of flowers like these will prevent them from curling.

Florists' Tape is a narrow somewhat sticky tape, usually green or brown, that comes in a small roll. As you use it, the warmth of your hands increases the adhesive quality. Use this tape to cover the false stems of dried flowers, or to wind around the stems of flowers when making a corsage. You can also use it to fasten water picks or pill bottles to sticks. When using a pinholder in a glass bowl, it is important to conceal the pins because they will be magnified by the glass. To do this, wind green tape around the outside of the circle of pins.

Daisy Tape is similar in looks to florists' tape but it is drier. It is usually white or a neutral color. You can crisscross it over Oasis at the top of a container to keep it in place, or you can use it to fasten a block of Oasis to a flat surface.

Hardware Cloth

This is somewhat similar to wire netting and can also be purchased at hardware stores. It is made of very heavy wire with small square openings. It is quite stiff and can be cut into shapes to use as bases for garlands and swags. It is strong enough to hold its shape even when greens or other decorative material are wired to it. I have found it particularly useful for fastening a piece of driftwood or a heavy branch to a pinholder. To do this, cut a strip of hardware cloth large enough to tack around the bottom three or four inches of the wood or branch, with an extra inch and a half to extend beyond, then you can fasten this extra bit securely into a heavy pinholder.

Plaster of Paris

This has a use similar to hardware cloth. You may have some pieces of branch coral, a heavy weathered branch, or something similar that is not suitable for using hardware cloth. Get some plaster of Paris and mix it according to directions. Then take a flat can the proper size for the base of your material, place the end of your branch or whatever in the can, and pour the plaster of Paris around it. When it hardens, your material will stand up permanently.

Wedge Holders

Wedge holders are flat, cone-shaped metal containers fastened to a long spike. For rooms with high ceilings, a church, or a ballroom, you may want very tall arrangements. Fill these wedge-shaped containers with additional flowers and add them to an arrangement to make it taller by means of the long spike, which is easily concealed.

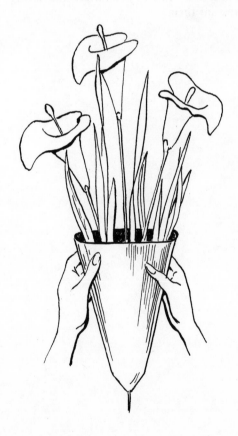

Wedge holders filled with Oasis hold flowers to add height to an arrangement. These are especially valuable with narrow-necked vases such as altar vases.

Aids for Tall Vases

There are several ways to fill a tall vase so that when you put flowers in it they will stay in position and not fall toward the edges, leaving a hole in the middle:

1. One that we have already mentioned is to fill the container with crumpled Oasis.
2. Another way is to fill the vase three-quarters full of damp sand and place a pinholder on top of the sand.
3. Another that is readily available to most people is to completely fill the container with upright pieces of privet, fern, yew, hemlock, or other greens. Cut off the tops level with the mouth of the container. Now when you insert the flowers they will stay where you want them.

A mass arrangement that illustrates the principles of design described in the text on pages 6 through 9. *Photo by Denby Versfeld Associates. Arrangement by Katherine N. Cutler.*

A Zulu water jug, petrified seaweed from an African beach, and flowers made from seedpods by native African women are dramatized against a simulated South African sunset. *Photo by Denby Versfeld Associates. Arrangement by Katherine N. Cutler.*

Modern Ikebana arrangement. *Arrangement by Kitten Ellison.*

Arrangement of foliage in tones of green and yellow to complement an antique brass container. *Photo by Denby Versfeld Associates. Arrangement by Kate Bogle.*

Altar arrangements made to flank a cross. Grapes and wheat are used to symbolize sacramental bread and wine. *Photo by Denby Versfeld Associates. Arrangement by Katherine N. Cutler.*

An arrangement of fruit and vegetables brightens an inviting kitchen corner. *Photo by Denby Versfeld Associates. Arrangement by Kate Bogel.*

In order to have a large centerpiece for a formal dinner table that will be low enough not to obstruct the guests view of each other, and still be in good proportion, the arrangement is extended at the sides, thereby allowing the height to be shortened. *Photo by Denby Versfeld Associates. Arrangement by Katherine N. Cutler.*

Containers,
Bases, and Accessories

Many beautiful vases, or *containers* as they are usually referred to in flower-arranging circles, are sold specifically to hold flowers. However, you are not limited to these. Sometimes an object designed for another purpose is the most attractive and the most fun to use. An antique china or pewter sugar bowl, a copper pitcher, a Bristol-glass perfume bottle, a footed water goblet, a wooden or metal box, or a Tole bread tray, all make lovely containers. Or try a natural object like a shell or a piece of driftwood. These are but a few of the many things that would lend their own interest to an arrangement.

**Antiques
and
Flea Market
Finds**

Looking for interesting containers should appeal to people who like to go antiquing. Some of the most-treasured containers come from antique shops, and they aren't necessarily expensive. For instance, if you come across an urn-shaped Victorian stove top, grab it. Inverted, it makes a footed urn that you will find just right for many types of arrangements. You might find an antique perfume bottle that you can buy for little money because it has lost its stopper. If you see a tall tea caddy, instead of making it into a lamp use it for a container for tall flowering branches. An old soup tureen is a fine container for flowers for a dining table. You may even find a chipped Victorian vase that would be very expensive if it were undamaged. The chipped places are easily hidden with leaves.

Try to be aware of commercial containers that would make interesting vases. One winter, on a ship going to South America, we had some Chilean wine at the table. The bottles were such a lovely shade of green and such a fascinating squat shape that I couldn't bear to think of them being thrown out, so I asked the steward to save them for me. At the time I had no idea what I would do with them. Now, filled with sprays of tradescantia, they make a decoration in my study, where they are placed asymmetrically on dark green brackets against the wall. Paint buckets, sprayed different colors, are fine for large arrangements, and in a later section I will tell about a unique use for tin cans.

Be on the lookout at rummage and white elephant sales for containers that may be a hideous color or too "busy" with decoration, but are of basically good design. You can take them home and paint them with a good flat paint. You can use any color, but one of my favorites is Satin Black which gives a dull, smooth finish. With good design and imagination you can transform an ugly vase into an elegant one.

Flowers and containers must never compete for interest. Each should complement the other for a harmonious effect. For this reason, it is difficult to use a container that is strong in color or is heavily decorated. The happiest choices are potteries in neutral shades of white, gray, and soft green, or metals such as iron, pewter, silver, copper, or brass. Black is always a good color and, like the "basic black dress," fits many occasions.

Every flower arranger will eventually have a favorite container—one for which she has many uses and one which never fails to inspire her. I have two, and I didn't search for either of them; they just happened. One is an alabaster epergne, and the other is a bronze container; both are featured in the color section.

Each year an antique show is held at our church, and some of us make arrangements to decorate the booths. One evening at the close of the show I was collecting my things and saw one of the dealers beginning to pack an alabaster epergne. It was love at first sight. I thought, "Oh, I must have that," never dreaming it would be in my price range. Evidently, though, the dealer was tired, and it was one thing less to pack and lug back to his store because he quoted me a ridiculously low figure and the epergne was mine. This is a "special occasion" container. I have used it in many flower shows with fruit and flowers, and it has been a "guest" at numerous parties. Arranged with live greens and cascading Christmas tree ornaments, it has become as much a part of our usual Christmas as the tree, and if I try to skip a year the family protests. For each of my daughters' weddings, instead of a tiered cake I had a large round one made with a hole in the center. The base of the epergne fit into the hole, and its tiers, decorated with stephanotis and gardenias and tiny ivy, acted as tiers of a cake.

My other favorite container which I use every day, I discovered out of desperation. I had been invited to do an arrangement for a large State Flower Show, which was in the form of an "Open House Show." My assignment was in the country house of an internationally famous hostess. I was told to do an arrangement on the piano in the drawing room. The specification said that an original Renoir in shades of pink and rose hung over the piano that was flanked by two armchairs covered in dull gold satin.

Frankly, I was at my wit's end. I knew the arrangement must be tall; that it must complement, not compete with, the picture; and that the container must be beautiful and distinctive. I didn't have one that I thought was just right, and I didn't want to buy one. One day I came into the garage and stumbled over a large black object. It was a metal lamp and shade. When my husband, who had been clearing out his father's attic, brought it home I took one look and said, "Ugh! Take it away." Now, as I moved it out of the way I noticed the shape of the base and thought, "That looks quite interesting." I removed the top

Containers

and shade and took the base into the house and started to polish it. I discovered it was bronze with a lovely soft patina. As the accumulation of dirt and grime was removed, the raised pattern of a bird sitting on a flowering spring branch emerged. With each rub of the polishing cloth I was more thrilled, and when it was finally finished it was beautiful. I had my distinctive container. Not only that, but the flowering branch gave me a clue for the arrangement. I would use apple blossoms.

I did just that—making a line arrangement, whose branching arms framed the picture without competing with it. For a focal point I used deep pink Martha Washington geraniums. An added bonus was that outside the window, on the day of the show, was an apple orchard in full bloom.

The best part about that experience is that from that day on the container has been in constant use in my own living room. It lends itself to line, mass, and line mass arrangements. And this brings up an important point. Some people feel that they must have many containers so that they can do different types of arrangements. I think it is more satisfactory to have a few containers that really appeal to you; learn to do different types of arrangements in them. One container can be surprisingly versatile.

With a little imagination and ingenuity, an object that was never planned to house flowers can become an exciting container for an arrangement. And you might make use of a favorite item that would otherwise be discarded or neglected. Here are a few ideas for containers that were not originally made for flowers:

sugar bowl	wine bottle
teapot	paint bucket
goblet	tin can
tea caddy	basket
Victorian stove top	pepper shaker
bread tray	shell
pitcher	driftwood
candlestick	palm spathe
bamboo	pumpkin
root	coral
gourds	cocoanut shell

In flower-arranging classes, I have asked pupils to bring containers that they find a problem to use, and they have brought three types so consistently that I think they must be a problem for many beginners. In each case the proper mechanics is the answer.

The first of these types is the widemouthed vase, I call it "the wedding-present vase," because almost every bride receives one. Let's look at how to solve this one:

a. A typical wedding-present vase. The creamy stock is a good choice in color and texture, but there is otherwise no integration of flowers and container.

b. The vase is placed on an upside-down saucer of the same porcelain as a base, adding more height. The vase does not dominate the flowers. A wedge of Oasis in the neck supports the flowers in a vertical design. More foliage is added and the stock is cut in varying lengths. *Photo by Denby Versfeld Associates. Arrangement by Katherine N. Cutler.*

Problem: Because of the wide mouth of the container (see photo), any flowers placed in it fall toward the rim, giving a very top-heavy effect and making it almost impossible to create good design. It is necessary to find a way to make the stems stay where you want them.

Solution: Wedge a piece of Oasis into the wide part of the container until it is held firmly by the narrower part of the vase. (You could also do this by filling the container with straight pieces of privet or other material, as described in the section on Mechanical Aids.) Once you know that your flower stems will stay where you place them, you can plan your design.

Problem: The second type that seems to give difficulty is the high, widemouthed bowl like a Revere bowl. Usually the large bowl is to be used for a mass arrangement on a table, and the problem is how to fill the cavity from one pinholder in the center.

Solution: In this case I definitely recommend using Oasis. A mass arrangement in this type bowl is one of the easiest of all to do if you have a large block of Oasis. Not only can you insert flower stems in the center but toward the edges of the bowl as well, and if the Oasis is a little higher than the rim, you can have the flowers swooping gracefully at the sides by inserting the stems at an angle.

The third most common problem is with glass containers. I have devoted a short section to this subject.

Glass Containers

Most expert arrangers agree that a glass container is one of the most difficult to use, and they avoid them whenever possible. One of the questions most frequently asked about them is, "How do you arrange flowers in a glass container when there is no way of concealing the stems?"

The answer is to make use of the stems in the design, rather than try to conceal them. If no stems show, the arrangement of flowers will look as though it is disembodied or floating in air. To make the stem design, first make sure that the stem or stems are stripped of foliage and reach to the center spot of the container bottom. Insert the other stem or stems at an angle, touching each side of the container, making a triangular pattern. This complements the triangular arrangement of the flowers.

In a *low glass bowl,* fasten a dry pinholder to the dry bottom of a container with Stickum. Wind green Daisy tape around the pins so that they will be hidden and not magnified by the glass. Conceal the pinholder with some decorative bits of foliage like rose or ivy.

If you are using a *tall glass bud vase* with a single rose, make sure that the stem is long enough to reach the bottom and still have enough height above the vase to be in good proportion. A spray of rose foliage may be left on the stem to be seen in the water through the glass.

Often a flower arrangement is greatly improved by putting it on a base. When would this be desirable? Perhaps when you have completed an arrangement, you feel that it lacks bottom weight. You can remedy this by putting the container on a base, making sure that it is suitable in color, size, and shape. A base may be any shape—round, rectangular, square, free form, and so on. When a base is used, it is considered a part of the container and therefore should integrate with it. The more experienced you become in arranging, the more you know intuitively when a base is needed. For instance, if you have made an arrangement in a round bowl, the horizontal line of a rectangular base gives an interesting contrast; and a piece of marble used as a base adds elegance to a beautiful Period container.

A base can literally raise the height of an arrangement; and a colored one can moderate or increase color in the design.

Arrangement in a glass vase

Bases and Accompanying Containers

Bases	Containers
Wood—painted, covered with fabric or plastic paper	Wooden, ceramic, basket, driftwood
	Metal, ceramic, cup
Slate	Tall Oriental vase
Oriental round	Flat rectangular container
Oriental scroll (flat)	Wooden, basket, ceramic
Bamboo mat	Fine porcelain, elegant Period containers
Marble	
Silver trivets, trays, inverted bowls	Silver bowls, candlesticks, vases
Gilt	Containers with gold tracings
Mirror	Glass containers

Helpful Hints for Containers

1. Copper and brass containers, although beautiful when polished, are sometimes used unpolished, when arrangement is complemented by dull finish.
2. Silver containers should always be polished.
3. Alabaster containers should be coated with melted paraffin as water causes alabaster to disintegrate.
4. Pinholders used in silver should be fastened to container with melted paraffin as Stickum will tarnish it.
5. Holes in the bottom of antique containers such as a lamp base may be plugged with a ball of Stickum.
6. Containers of good design but unattractive decoration may be spray-painted a solid color.
7. Paint buckets, bread pans, inexpensive paper-mache containers can be spray-painted and used when many containers are required to decorate tables for a large group.
8. Pumpkins or large squash may be hollowed out and used as containers for decorative foliage.

Collecting
Accessories

One of the fascinating sidelines of flower arranging is "collecting," and the woods and beaches are full of wonderful things for the flower arranger to find. I have some shelves in the garage where I keep my collection. There are jars of smooth white, pink, gray, and black pebbles gathered on daily walks along the beach. These are useful for concealing pinholders and for holding bulbs in place when they are growing indoors in a bowl. Usually only white pebbles are used for this, but you can achieve a really dramatic effect by using white narcissus surrounded by coal-black pebbles in a low white bowl, or pink hyacinths held in place by silvery-gray stones in a pewter container. Incidentally, it is wise to gather things on a beach the moment you see them. I didn't realize until I lived at the shore that the sea is not consistent in giving up its treasures. One day the beach may be covered with white pebbles and then, for days you may see only scattered ones, their place being taken by blue and black mussel shells or tiny white clamshells.

On my shelf there are jagged pieces of slag, useful for concealing pinholders and adding color and design to an arrangement when used as accessories. One is black, shot with streaks of turquoise. This came from the site of an iron furnace in the Berkshires which, legend has it, supplied the iron for guns of the *Monitor* in the Civil War. I found other pieces on a municipal dump near a factory where glass Christmas balls are made. Some of these pieces look like white rock candy and others look like foaming blue-green tropical water that has been caught in motion and solidified. They have been just right as accessories for flower show interpretative arrangements relating to the sea. In Bermuda I have found sand-flecked pieces of pink coral, which complement many arrangements, and bags of casuarina cones—tiny perfect cones less than half an inch long—that are invaluable in making wreaths with dried material at Christmas. When my husband and I travel, we leave with respectable, conventional luggage—but our return! When our luggage is placed on the pier, it is surrounded by paper shopping bags, straw valises, string-tied cartons—anything that will hold my collection. Also, my husband has become accustomed to the fact that we not only have to have a customs inspector but an agricultural inspector as well. While he and the customs inspector attend to the regular luggage, the agricultural inspector and I go into a huddle. He sorts carefully through my treasures, confiscating some, but allowing me to keep most of them. Once one held up a cocoanut spathe and said, "What on earth are you going to do with this?" Already visualizing the arrangement, I launched into a description complete with gestures. He looked at me quizzically for a minute, thrust it into my hand and said, "Here, take it and have fun."

As a result of these trips I have added to my collection of white pebbles, but these are very special ones of sparkling marble, picked up in shallow water off the island of Delos in Greece. I have pieces of pink granite from the ruins in Baalbek, Lebanon, and yellow sandstone taken from the desert in front of the Sphinx. In Sicily as I arrived back at the ship, by taxi, from a picnic on the beach at Taormina, a local policeman helped me unload a heavy plastic bag. His curiosity got the better of him, and when he looked inside and saw it filled with rose-pink stones, he was very amused and called some of his colleagues to come over and look. I'm sure he was thinking, "These crazy Americans!" Not so crazy really because I have used those stones many times.

On a visit to a kibbutz in Israel I found some large, round, flat pods under a tree that I had never seen before, and on the campus of the American University in Beirut I gathered the peanut-shaped pods of the mescal bean tree. I also have stiff cones from a cedar of Lebanon, and some small, round, smooth, hard ones from a tree on the island of Malta. All of these pods and cones will be in my Christmas wreath.

On a picnic at the Cape of Good Hope our car got stuck in the sand, and as it was being freed I wandered down the beach and found the most incredible pieces of wood—ebony black and twisted into fantastic shapes. Later in the week I bought, literally from the head of a Zulu woman, one of the homemade black clay pots they use for cooking. The combination of the twisted wood and the black pot never fails to cause enthusiastic comment. Smooth black stones from a beach on the island of Nuka Hiva, in the South Seas, form a "river" in my Japanese garden. Not only do all these things give me pleasure to use, but they bring back memories of so many wonderful days!

Storage

One word of caution! Keep your collection in order. Otherwise, things get in such a jumble that you either throw them away in sheer annoyance, or are unable to find something when you need it most. I keep small stones sorted by color in glass jars. Larger stones and slag are placed on the open shelves. Cones, sorted by size, are hung from nails in heavy shopping bags. Driftwood and weathered wood are placed on the shelves. Branches of dried material are tied with heavy twine and hung from nails.

It is convenient to keep a mental note of your friends' collections, you never know when you might want to borrow something. One of my friends found some dried black sunflower heads with lovely curved stems on a debris heap. Not only has she used them successfully in arrangements but has generously lent them to other arrangers. These were used in an arrangement described in a later section in this book.

In addition to natural objects, be on the lookout for figurines, statuettes, or decorative sculpture that can be used to dramatize an arrangement.

2
Different Types of Arrangements

Foliage
Arrangements

Probably the greatest wealth of material available to flower arrangers, whether they live in the East, West, North, or South—in a city, village, town, or open country—is foliage. Leaves and branches from trees, bushes, vines, and house plants come in so many shapes, sizes, colors, and textures that the possibilities for interesting arrangements are endless.

In the northern part of the country, from earliest spring when the first curling shoots of fern and skunk cabbage appear in the woods until late fall when the last oak leaves fall from the trees, there is a great variety and abundance.

You can use branches of beech, oak, maple, or hickory. You may have a bouquet from your dooryard of laurel, andromeda, ivy, or juniper or one from the vegetable garden of rhubarb, kale, broccoli, spinach, or beet leaves. House plants are also a never-ending source, with the tall leaves of sansevieria or dracaena often forming the basis for a striking arrangement, and begonia, philodendron, or cyclamen leaves making a focal point.

The southern part of the country abounds in wonderful foliage. There are sansevieria, sago palm, palmetto, philodendron, loquat, pittosporum, podocarpus, and much more.

Although we are apt to think of foliage as being green—and it is true that much of it is in that shade—there is a surprisingly wide color range. There are yellow, scarlet, and orange maple leaves, the golden leaves of hickory, and the red and bronze ones of oak. If you keep your eyes open, you're bound to be thrilled by an unexpected color. This happened to me this fall, when I discovered some leaves on a hydrangea bush that were a beautiful clear bright blue.

Color Accents on Green

Yellow and Orange	Bronze	Violet	Red	White
Coleus	Andromeda	Canna	Azalea	Caladium
Croton	Beech	Coleus	Beet	Dieffenbachia
Pothos	Galax	Hydrangea	Begonia	Dracaena
Sansevieria	Juniper	Ti	Caladium	Euphorbia
Variegated	Leucothoë	Tradescantia	Coleus	Holly
Euonymous	Magnolia		Dogwood	Hosta
Yellow Privet	Peony		Echeveria	Tradescantia
Pandanus	Sea Grape		Peony	Variegated
	Hydrangea		Rose	Holly
				Variegated
				Ivy
				Pandanus

**Selecting
and
Cutting
Foliage**

When you cut foliage from your plants for arrangements, you are really helping them because proper pruning not only improves the shape of the plant but is beneficial to its growth. Select branches that will fit in your visualized arrangement. You will find the most interesting shapes at the bottom of a bush where they are reaching for light. Cut with a sharp instrument so that you don't leave a jagged area that is susceptible to decay.

Form

Round and Heart-shaped	Spiky	Pendulant	Irregular
Cabbage	Aspidistra	Clematis	Begonia
Caladium	Broom	Grape Ivy	(several)
Eucalyptus	Canna	Ivy	Ivy
Galax	Dracaena	Ivy Geranium	Maple
Geranium	Fern	Kangaroo Vine	Nephthytis
Hen and Chicken	Iris	Passion Vine	Philodendron
Hosta	Juniper	Philodendron	(several)
Palmetto	Pittosporum	Pothos	
Philodendron	Podocarpus	Smilax	
Pothos	Sago Palm	Tradescantia	
Sea Grape	Sansevieria		
Violet	Ti		
	Yucca		

If you live in an area where the winter is severe, it is best to cut foliage like rhododendron and holly, whose leaves curl because of low temperatures, before it gets extremely cold. The foliage will last a long time, particularly if you keep it in a cool place.

As with flowers, foliage should be put in deep water for several hours before arranging. Some leaves like to be completely immersed. If you are doubtful as to whether a particular kind needs it, go ahead and cover it with water in your sink or laundry tub. Some that definitely *do* need this are listed in the section on *Conditioning*.

Shaping Foliage

If you wish to have tall sweeping curves as the basis for your arrangement, foliage can be manipulated prior to using it. You can do this for sprays such as podocarpus or broom by using wire. (For details, see page 32.)

Gently bend leaves such as aspidistra, iris, or sansevieria by massaging them along the center with your fingertips. The heat from your hand will make them pliable. Smaller leaves like those of narcissus or tulips can be curled around your index finger. In stubborn cases you can fasten a leaf into a roll with Scotch Tape. When you remove the tape the leaf will spring back into a curve. You can cut palmetto into a desired shape. Stiff materials like palm, pods, and bark can be scalded or boiled to make them pliable.

Uses for Foliage Arrangements

Foliage arrangements are good for many reasons. In the first place, they are extremely long-lasting. They are lovely in themselves but can also be the background for one or two added flowers. Material is easily available for a large mass arrangement, or you can have an eye-capturing one with only three beautifully curved large leaves. Foliage arrangements are a wise choice for modern or contemporary houses as the bold, clean-cut lines of some varieties make an attractive silhouette against the expanses of glass or plain walls, and blend with the streamlined furnishings. Foliage is used in a restrained manner in Oriental arrangements, which we will discuss in the section on *Ikebana*. As brilliant colors usually surround the outside of Spanish-type houses in the South and West, it is restful and cool to use inside arrangements in all shades and color intensities of green.

During the hot spells that come in summer, it would be refreshing to see the fireplace filled with masses of rhododendron, laurel, or fern; and on a cold day the same fireplace might display a simulated fire of scarlet and gold autumn leaves. When you use autumn leaves it is smart to take a lesson from nature: Just as the leaves seem more brilliant on the hillsides because they are interspersed with evergreens, arrangements using these leaves are more effective when dark green foliage is added.

Because leaves and branches are so typical of the outdoors, naturalistic containers are especially suited to them. Interesting pieces of driftwood, lichen-covered tree stumps, or a weathered root are good choices. You can make foliage arrangements, using a cup pinholder on a flat rock, a burl, or a piece of polished wood. Conventional containers can be used too. Those of wood, like a bowl, a mortar, or a square pillow vase, are all good. I recently saw an unusual one made by a schoolchild by winding twine closely around a fruit-juice can and then shellacking it.

An accessory is often used with a foliage arrangement to complete the outdoor mood or to continue the line of the design. For instance, the figure of a squirrel, properly placed at the base of leafed branches, would suggest the woods. Or the curved wings of a duck might be the touch needed to complete a curved line in an arrangement. You might use an unusual rock at the base of another arrangement to give visual weight and stability. Whatever you choose, be sure that it blends with the arrangement in suitability, scale, color, and texture so that it becomes an integral part of the whole.

Foliage Useful for Arrangements

Name	Description	Where found
Andromeda (an-*drom*eda)	Evergreen. Clusters of leaves that are bronze, red, or chartreuse depending on season.	Widely grown shrub. Suitable for dooryard planting.
Artemisia (ar-teh-*mee*-seea)	Gray- or ivory-colored. Soft, feathery spikes.	Gardens. Florist.
Aspidistra (ass-pi-*dis*tra)	Long wide leaf, one to two feet long, tapered at end. Rich green.	Easily grown house plant, or from florist.
Azalea (a-*zay*-lee-a)	Clusters of tiny shiny dark green leaves on stiff stem. Turns red in autumn.	Widely grown shrub. Suitable for dooryard planting.

Name	Description	Where found
Beech	Copper- or purple-colored oval leaves of large tree. Graceful branches.	Widely grown in the United States.
Begonia (bee-*go*-nee-a)	Leaves of many shapes depending on variety.	Grown in warm climates. Good as house plant.
Billbergia (bill-*burr*-gia)	Blue-green pineapple-like leaves.	Florist.
Caladium (cal-*ade*-ee-um*)	Large heart-shaped leaves. Pink and green, white and green.	Grown in tropical climates. House plant.
Calla	Large leathery arrow-shaped green leaves.	Grows in warm climates. Florist.
Camellia (ka-*meal*-ee-a)	Dark green glossy leaves alternating on sturdy stem.	Grown outdoors in South and West. Florist.
Canna	Long wide tapering leaves tinged with red or violet.	Widely grown outdoors in the United States.
Carnation	Feathery blue-green spirals from sheath.	Grows in temperate and warm climates. Florist.
Catbrier	Like large-leafed smilax.	Grows wild in many states.
Cedrus Atlantica (*seed*-rus-at-*lan*-tee-ka)	Evergreen tree. Blue-green needles in tiny rosettes along branch.	Grows in Northeast. Cut at some florists'.
Clematis (*klem*-ah-tis)	Climbing plant. Grows in beautiful curves.	Grows outdoors except far North.
Coleus (*ko*-lee-us)	Pointed leaves alternating on short stem, ending in cluster. Yellow, chartreuse, pink, red, purple, variegated. Condition by putting stems in hot water.	Grows in gardens or as a house plant.

Name	Description	Where found
Croton (*kro*-ton)	Long narrow leaves from four to eighteen inches. Others broad, some spiral. Many colors.	Grows outdoors in warm climates. Florist.
Cyclamen (*sigh*-clomen)	Small heart-shaped leaves. Green. Marked and veined with lighter green.	House plant.
Dieffenbachia (deef-en-*bock*-ia)	Large wide tapered leaves. Green. Spotted or veined with white. Individual leaves used.	Tropical climates. House plant.
Dracaena (drah-*see*-na)	Large wide curved leaves. Green and yellow, green and white.	Outdoors in tropical climates. House plant.
Eucalyptus (you-ka-*lip*-tus)	Gray-blue-green leaves grow in spirals on long stem.	Trees in tropical and semitropical climates. Florist.
Euonymous (you-*on*-ee-muss)	Small glossy leaves grow closely on leathery stem. Grows as bush or vine. Evergreen.	Grows outdoors many states. Suitable for foundation planting.
Euphorbia or Snow on the Mountain (you-*for*-bee-a)	Low growing. Small green leaves edged with white. Grow in clusters.	Widely grown in gardens.
Ferns, many varieties	Many shapes. Feathers. Sword-shaped. Lacy.	Grows wild or as house plant.
Galax (*gay*-lax)	Large round or heart-shaped leaves. Leathery texture. Stiff short stem.	Grows in eastern and southeastern North America.
Geranium	Ruffly, velvety, round green leaves.	Grows widely outdoors. House plant.
Hickory	Leaves of forest tree, golden in autumn.	Native American tree.

Name	*Description*	*Where found*
Holly	Dark-green or green-and-white glossy spiny leaves and red berries grow along woody stems and branches.	Grows widely in the United States. Florist.
Hosta or Funkia	Blue-green, green, or green-and-white. Some leaves large and heart-shaped. Others long, curved, and pointed. Individual leaves used.	Widely grown in gardens.
Huckleberry	Flat dark green leaves growing flat on woody stem.	Grows wild in North America. Often included with flowers from florist.
Ilex (*eye*-lex)	Tiny smooth dark green leaves growing densely on stem. Evergreen. Small branches.	Suitable for foundation planting.
Ivy	Climbing plant. Five-pointed leaf. Graceful sprays.	Widely grown.
Ivy Geranium	Grows in cascading sprays from flowering plant. Leaf similar to ivy.	Grows widely in warm climates or as house plant.
Juniper	Evergreen. Feathery plume-like sprays with gray-blue berries. Some varieties turn bronze in fall.	Suitable for dooryard planting.
Laurel	Evergreen shrub. Oval pointed leaves grow in clusters on stiff stem. Clusters good in fruit arrangements.	Suitable for dooryard planting. Grows wild in many parts of country.

Name	Description	Where found
Leucothoë (Loo-*kŏth*-o-ee)	Evergreen. Pointed leaves alternating on wandlike stem. Leathery texture. Color changes at different seasons from green to purplish-green, bronze, and chartreuse.	Grows widely. Suitable for dooryard planting. Cut stems as soon as bloom is finished. New stems will follow.
Loquat (*low*-kwat)	Small evergreen shrub tree. Strong dark green leaves growing in clusters.	Grows in semitropics.
Magnolia	Large green oval leaves. Some have brown on underside. Good for preserving with glycerin. Used as branches or individual leaves.	Widely grown in the southern United States. Florist.
Mahonia (Mah-*hoe*-nee-a)	Low-growing evergreen shrub with green or bronze hollylike leaf.	Suitable for foundation planting.
Maple	Native forest tree. In fall various colors of red, yellow, and orange.	Grows widely.
Oak	Native forest tree. Leaves red or brown in autumn.	Grows widely. Florist.
Pachysandra (pack-i-*san*-dra)	Low growing. Serrated green leaves in clusters on soft stem.	Widely grown as ground cover.
Pandanus (pan-*day*-nus)	Long swordlike leaves. Green, striped with yellow or white.	Grows in warm climates or as house plant.
Philodendron (fill-oh-*den*-dron)	Many varieties and shapes. Graceful sprays. Individual leaves.	Grows in warm climates. House plants.
Pine	Evergreen tree. Needled branches.	Grows widely.

Name	*Description*	*Where found*
Pittosporum (pitt-*us*-pore-um)	Evergreen. Green oval leaves grow in rosettes.	Grows in warm climates. Florist.
Podocarpus (poe-doe-*car*-puss)	Evergreen. Dark green featherlike plumes. Can be bent to graceful curves.	Grows to small tree in warm climates.
Privet	Small semi-evergreen leaves grow along woody stem. Used for hedges. Sometimes yellow.	Easily and widely grown.
Rhododendron (roe-doe-*den*-drun)	Dark green evergreen shrub. Long oval leaves growing in circle around branch. Good in large mass arrangements.	Widely grown. Suitable for foundation planting. Wild in many states.
Sansevieria (san-see-*vee*-ria)	Thick green swordlike leaf, one to four or five feet long. Some striped and marked with yellow.	Grows outdoors in warm climates. House plant.
Scotch Broom	Thin stringlike strands growing in plumes. Dark green. Easily shaped in curves.	Grows widely as outdoor bush. Florist.
Sea Grape	Large round leathery green leaves tinged with red or bronze. Used as single leaves.	Grows wild in southern states.
Ti (tee)	Long narrow tapering green leaves with red-violet edge.	Tropical. Florist.
Violet	Low-growing heart-shaped leaves.	Grows wild and in gardens.
Yew	Very dark green, low-growing evergreen shrub. Small needles an inch long grow flat on branches.	Suitable for foundation planting.

cArrangements of Flowering Shrubs, Vines, and Trees

Most people think of garden flowers, wildflowers, or those purchased from a florist, when they plan arrangements, but some of the loveliest flowers are those of flowering shrubs, climbing vines, fruit trees, and other trees.

One woman I know has recently done a very clever thing. In her seventies, and suffering from arthritis, she has had her lovely garden changed from one of annuals and perennials to a garden of shrubs, vines, and flowering trees. "You know," she said, "I have always loved wandering around the garden and getting inspiration for my arrangements by cutting flowers when I see them growing. It isn't at all the same when plant material is brought to you already cut. So, since I can no longer stoop over, I am having my flowers at a level where I don't have to bend."

As a result she has a cutting garden from earliest spring, when she can force flowering branches, until late in the fall and winter, when some of the berry-bearing shrubs are at their loveliest. And among these things is a wealth of flower forms to make lovely arrangements.

If you would like to cultivate some shrubs, trees, and vines, here is a list of a few that will give you beautiful arrangement material.

Shrubs

ABELIA: This is a handsome semi-evergreen with small-leafed foliage. Small tubular flowers in white, pink, or rose bloom on it all summer. When the flowers drop in the fall, attractive clusters of dusty rose bracts are left. This grows in mild climates as far north as southern New England.

BRIDAL WREATH (*Spiraea*): In the spring, round clusters of tiny white flowers bloom all along arching branches.

BUTTERFLY BUSH (*Buddleia*): Spikes of lavender and purple flowers that are fragrant and bloom in the summer. It was given its common name because it attracts butterflies.

CAMELLIA: Glossy green leaves and showy large single, semidouble and double flowers of white and many shades of pink and red on a tall bush. Grows mostly in South and West, but with protection will grow as far north as New Jersey.

CEANOTHUS: Lovely clusters of flowers in shades of blue. Grows in Pacific coast area. A collection of different varieties will give bloom from spring until fall.

COTONEASTER: Low-growing shrub with attractive growth of branches and colorful berries in the fall. The small leaves turn a lovely red in the fall. Grows in temperate regions and hardy quite far north.

FIRE THORN (*Pyracantha*): This is particularly successful for espaliering. The small white flowers that appear in summer are insignificant, but are followed in the fall by gorgeous orange-red berries that last all winter. Loved by birds.

FLOWERING ALMOND (*Prunus*): Stems covered with small pink and white blossoms resembling button chrysanthemums. Blooms in early spring in temperate zones.

FORSYTHIA: Deep yellow bell-shaped flowers circle wandlike branches in March and April. Leaves appear after flowers drop. Not uncommon to see them blooming in a late snowstorm.

HIBISCUS: More interesting for flowers than foliage. Flowers a circle of large petals in lovely colors—pink, red, apricot—bloom in all seasons in warm climates. Flower heads will last for a day out of water. The large bushes are often used for hedges.

HYDRANGEA: Bushes with large flower heads composed of clusters of tiny blossoms of blue, pink, and green-white. Flowers last all summer. In the fall turn to shades of lavender, blue-green, green, and bronze. Dry beautifully. Bloom in temperate climates.

JAPANESE QUINCE: Blossoms appear before leaves in early spring, on woody bush. Flowers are like tiny wild roses colored rose-red (delicate pink when forced). Grows in Northeast. Small fruits are not edible but give a delightful fragrance to bureau drawers, closets.

LILAC: One of the most loved shrubs. Tall bushes with terminal bushy pyramids of flower heads in shades of purple, pinky-lavender, rose, and white. They have a delightful fragrance. Many hybrid varieties. Grow in the Northeast.

MOCK ORANGE (*Philadelphus*): This shrub probably got its common name because its fragrance is similar to that of orange blossoms. It is sometimes mistakenly called *Syringa*. The small satiny white flowers with prominent orange stamens grow on pliant branches. It blooms in June in the Northeast.

SNOWBERRY (*Symphoricarpos*): Attractive for its clusters of globular waxy berries in the fall, which last for several months. Grows widely.

STEWARTIA: Has large white or cream-colored flowers like single roses, which bloom all summer along the Atlantic coast. An outstanding shrub, not commonly planted.

VITEX: Grows outdoors in warm climates and as far north as southern New England. Has slender spiky terminal blue-purple flower heads. Blooms in late August and September.

Many kinds of vines and shrubs such as the acuba, pachysandra, ivy, and philodendron used here can be placed on a pinholder in water where they will grow roots. In a container such as the brass box shown here, they can be enjoyed as an arrangement until the roots are large enough to plant. *Photo by Denby Versfeld Associates. Arrangement by Katherine N. Cutler.*

Flowering Vines

BITTERSWEET: Vigorous hardy climbing vines, suitable for walls and fences. Valued for arrangements because of the yellow berries which pop open in the fall to expose bright red seeds inside. Also grows wild but is on conservation lists except when owner grown.

CLEMATIS: This grows in temperate regions and is suitable for fences, trellises, or walls, There are many kinds, and it is possible to have a succession of bloom from spring to fall. According to variety, flowers are small or large. Many are fragrant. There are many colors —white, blue, lilac, rose, pink, yellow, and purple. The vines have tendrils that are graceful for arrangements.

CUP-AND-SAUCER (*Cobaea*): The common name is suggested by the large violet bell-shaped flowers with a large leafy calyx at the base. This is a good climber. In arrangements the flower is distinctive as is the dried calyx. Blooms in summer.

DUTCHMAN'S-PIPE (*Aristolochia*): This vine grows in warm climates. Has large heart-shaped leaves and pipe-shaped flowers. It blooms in June and July. Its value to the arranger is the unusually shaped flower and the seedpod which comes in the fall and looks like a tiny fluted upside-down parachute.

PASSIONFLOWER (*Passiflora*): This vine grows in warm climates, or indoors in the North. Has wide flat flowers in a mixture of blue, lavender and white, pink and red. The flowers are thought to be emblematic of the crucifixion of Christ. They are striking in formation, and the vines grow in fascinating tendrils.

TRUMPET VINE (*Campsis*): A strong climber, this vine has feathery leaves and funnel-shaped flowers of orange and red. Blooms in August and September in many parts of the country.

Flowering Trees

In addition to shrubs and vines there are many kinds of fruit trees, both those that bear edible fruit and ornamental ones, whose blossoms are beautiful for arrangements.

When you cut flowering branches, look for ones that are growing in interesting angles. By judicious pruning you can emphasize these. To arrange them you will need a heavy pinholder, and the pins *must* be sharp. If you make little crisscross cuts on the end of the branch, you can spread it into a brush and have a larger surface to stick on the pins. If you want the branch at an angle, it is best to jam it firmly on the pinholder in a vertical position and then push it to the angle you want, rather than impale it on the pinholder at an angle. If you use a tall vase, of course, a pinholder isn't necessary (see *Aids for Tall Vases,* page 36). Oasis is not practical for heavy branches, as their weight causes the wet Oasis to crumble.

Flowering branches are beautiful arranged by themselves. You might put Japanese quince in a tall black container like a tea caddy. The dull color is a dramatic contrast to the brilliant pink flowers. Apricot blossoms with their stark white flowers against black bark seem to call for a low, white container, while pussy willows are a natural for pewter.

If you want to use other flowers as an accent to flowering branches, it is attractive to use those that would naturally be growing at the same time. Some of these are tulips, daffodils, violets, crocuses, grape hyacinths, narcissus.

A lovely way to use flowering branches with other flowers is to make a *dish garden*. To do this:

1. Choose a low, flat container—a large plate, a platter, or a tray.
2. Fasten a cup pinholder, holding water, to the side or back of the container and arrange the flowering branches in it.
3. Beneath them, at scattered intervals, fasten flat-bottomed pill bottles of different sizes to the container with Stickum or florists' clay. Fill these with small bunches of appropriate small flowers suitable in scale. Wildflowers are pretty to use as well as the small garden ones.
4. Fill the spaces between the pill bottles with moss and natural-looking stones to hide the bottles.

The effect should be that of flowers growing naturally under a flowering bush. A dish garden like this will stay fresh for a long time if you keep topping the bottles and pinholder with water. A miniature version of an arrangement like this makes a charming gift.

Some of the most beautiful flowers for arrangements are those of large trees that are known mostly for their foliage. Often the flowers bloom so high that they go unnoticed. These flowers are doubly precious because they are available for such a short blooming time.

One of the most beautiful is that of the huge *tulip tree* (*liriodendron*). This is a forest tree of the Northeast and Middle West. In May and June it has exquisite bell-shaped flowers that are chartreuse green with a yellow-bordered salmon-pink interior. I saw a woman, at a flower show, look at an arrangement using some of these blossoms and heard her say, "I wonder what those exotic flowers are? They must have been sent from the tropics." I laughed to myself, because I knew that an hour earlier she had walked under a row of tulip trees in bloom on the golf course.

Another of my favorites is the blossom of the *Norway maple*. This tree lines many of our suburban streets and parkways. In the spring the flower is a spray like a miniature sky rocket of tiny yellow stars. Perhaps they are not used more as cut flowers because people seeing them casually mistake them for early foliage. But they *are* flowers that harden well and are beautiful in arrangements.

Many admire the tall pink or white candles of the *horse chestnut tree*. Perhaps because they grow so high, most people don't think to pick them. These are well worth finding a ladder and climbing to pick as they also harden well. Be sure to crush the end of the stems with a hammer so that there will be more area to absorb water. They make striking arrangements.

These are but a few examples of many of the flowers you will find on trees if you keep your "seeing eye" open.

Chartreuse Norway maple blossoms and daffodils are combined to make an arrangement that is the essence of spring. Note how the placement of the daffodils gives interest and dimension to the design. *Photo by Roche. Arrangement by Catherine H. Smith.*

Some Flowering Trees

DOGWOOD: This is found from Massachusetts to Florida. It is wonderful for arrangements in the spring, when it is white with what are mistakenly called flowers but are really waxy white bracts surrounding small green flower heads. These appear before the leaves and grow on flat branches. In the fall the center fruits are red and there is a reddish tint to the foliage. Although it is among the most beautiful plants for arrangements, it is on the conservation list in many states and should not be picked when growing wild. Fortunately, it is becoming one of the most popular cultivated trees.

FRUIT TREES: Almost all fruit trees have beautiful blossoms in the spring. Some, in addition to bearing edible fruit, have varieties that are grown for their ornamental blossoms like cherry and crab apple.

HORSE CHESTNUT: Grows widely over the United States. It has handsome upright stalks of flowers like huge candles. This is an impressive flower that is seen too seldom in arrangements. Mostly white or pink flowers, but some varieties may be yellow, purple, or red.

MOUNTAIN ASH: This tree grows in the northern part of the United States. It has sprays of white flowers in the spring, and clusters of orange and red berries in the fall. It is the berries, rather than the flowers, that are valuable for arrangements.

NORWAY MAPLE: This tree is common in most of the country. It is often seen as a border tree for streets or roads. In the spring it has showering sprays of tiny chartreuse flowers.

REDBUD TREE (*Cercis*): This tree, sometimes called the Judas tree, grows over most of temperate North America. It has red buds in winter, and in the spring, before the leaves appear, clusters of purple-rose flowers shaped like tiny sweet peas.

STAR MAGNOLIA (*Magnolia stellata*): This is a small tree with angular branches and is spectacular for white starlike flowers and long pointed buds, which appear before the leaves. Grows widely.

TULIP TREE: This is a forest tree of the Northeast and Middle West. Very tall. Exquisite bell-shaped flowers in spring.

**Forcing
Branches**

In parts of the country, where winter snow and cold make you long for spring, it is fun to cut branches of flowering shrubs, fruit trees, and other trees, and bring them into the house to force them into bloom. It is exciting in this way to extend their short blooming time.

About the earliest that you can force branches successfully is late January or early February. It will take from one to several weeks, depending on how close to the natural blooming time you cut them. However, if you cut branches that are interesting in shape, you can enjoy the linear pattern even before the buds begin to swell and the blossoms appear. Don't cut so many that the charm of the individual branch is lost.

On one of the mild days apt to come in the middle of winter, go out and see what you can find. There may be something from your dooryard like laurel, rhododendron, andromeda, azalea, or star magnolia, or something from the garden like forsythia or Japanese quince. In your yard you may get dogwood, Japanese maple, beech, birch, or horse chestnut. On a walk in the country keep your eyes open for pussy willow, swamp maple, witch hazel, spice bush, or alder. Fruit trees—apple, pear, cherry, apricot, plum, and crab apple—are all wonderful for forcing. The leaves and flowers have a delicacy in form and color that is enchanting.

To Force Branches

1. Cut branches of generous length with a sharp knife or pruning shears. Select those that are of medium thickness and avoid the ones that are twiggy.
2. After you have cut them, pound the ends of the stems with a hammer or slit them and peel back some of the bark so that they will absorb a maximum amount of water. If you cut the branches very early in the season, put them in the bathtub and cover them with tepid water overnight.
3. While they are forcing, put them in a deep container of water in a room with a temperature of 65°–70°. Your living room would probably be fine and they can be decorative.
4. Change the water frequently. As moisture helps the buds and flowers develop, spray them from time to time.

You can bring a corner of your garden into the house weeks ahead of time with an arrangement of forsythia and daffodils. Purple violets with pussy willows will make you long for a spring wildflower pilgrimage. And the tiny forced leaves of sweet gum branches, combined with the first curved shoots of skunk cabbage, will make you forget the March winds howling outside.

Fruit and Vegetable Arrangements

It is one thing to arrange fruit for eating in a bowl, and an entirely different matter to use it as material for a decorative arrangement. By all means have the family fruit bowl, but relegate it to an area where the family can nibble at will and it doesn't matter if removing an apple leaves a void or if a bunch of grapes becomes increasingly smaller.

Fruit and vegetables are very decorative. They come in a wide variety of form, color, and texture so that the possibilities for using them are endless—not only for conventional arrangements in dining rooms but for distinctive arrangements in other parts of the house. Bananas, pineapples, long-necked squash, and bunches of celery give *height;* apples, oranges, plums, limes, peaches, and pomegranates are *round* forms; pears, avocados, nectarines, persimmons, and plum tomatoes lend interest with their *triangular* and *eliptical* shapes. And bunches of grapes, bananas, peppers, and gourds are *curved.* You will find it interesting to combine these forms.

As for color, there is every color imaginable. Pineapples are not always brown and green—they also have rosy and orange tints. Pears can be brown, green, pink, or blush red. (If you want the latter color on a pear and it isn't there, rub your lipstick on it, smooth it in with your finger, and no one will know that it didn't grow that way!) Plums are green, flame, yellow, red, and purple. Apples are green, yellow, red, and chartreuse. You can make an arrangement in almost any color scheme.

To give your fruit arrangements distinction, learn to use material that is a little unusual. In the late spring tiny pineapples, only three or four inches long, with plumy green tops come on the market. These are too small to sell in food markets but are available through a florist and are charming to use. Pokeberry weed, which gives distinction with its clusters of purplish-black berries, is to be had for the picking, but if you do pick it, take a cigarette lighter with you to sear the stems. Often when a stem of bananas is delivered to a fruit market, there is a group of tiny undeveloped bananas at the top. These the dealer cuts off and throws away and they aren't seen by the general public. If you ask the dealer to save them for you, you will be delighted when you see what fun they are to use.

Osage oranges, the yellowish-green fruit of the maclura tree, add lovely color and interesting texture to arrangements. Try using kumquats in branches rather than singly. And if you know anyone who has a mandarin orange tree, beg, borrow, or steal some of the smallest, which are only an inch in diameter, like tiny tangerines.

When you go to a market to select fruit for an arrangement, don't feel that you have to buy it by the pound or dozen. If you only want one of this or two of that, put them in separate bags and have them weighed individually.

Everything that you use should be without blemish and sparkling clean. The best way to clean these fruits is to wash them and then rub them with waxed paper.

Accessories

Foliage with a leathery texture is good to use in fruit arrangements. It holds up better than some of the more delicate types and usually has glossy leaves which are in harmony with the shine of the fruit. Clusters of laurel will last well without being in water. To use them, hold the three or four leaves of the cluster tightly together and with your thumb and first two fingers insert the stem into a crevice between pieces of fruit. When you release them, the leaves will expand in a natural-looking way.

Leucothoë, green in summer and purply bronze in winter, is another excellent foliage to use. Pittosporum rosettes, sprigs of green and yellow privet, pieces of huckleberry are all helpful and can be used in water picks. Bold leaves like canna, sansevieria, aspidistra, and magnolia are useful for forming a bold design.

You are not limited to the conventional bowl or compote as a container. You could use a bread tray, a brass lamp base, scales, graduated boards like steps, footed bowls, silver cake baskets, or a bamboo mat.

In a symmetrical arrangement you could have each side end in a bunch of grapes hanging over the edge of the container. In an asymmetrical one or S curve, choose a bunch of grapes that in hanging over the side will curve to complete the reverse curve. It is easy to have a bunch of grapes hang free over the edge of a container: Wire a florists' pick to the stem at the top and then thrust the pointed end of the pick into a secure piece of fruit above.

If you want the effect of a bunch of grapes, and you don't happen to have one, you can wire clusters of cherries together or drill holes through the top of nuts and wire them into bunches. In the center of an arrangement, where they can lie on top of other fruit, you can get the effect of a bunch of grapes by using toothpicks to fasten fruit like cranberries, blackberries, or strawberries to the fruit below.

Let's see how to go about making a fruit arrangement. This will be a symmetrical-triangular design on an antique white compote with gold luster decoration. The fruits will be a pineapple, green and yellow apples, tangerines, limes, yellow pears, and bananas. You will need:

> A large pinholder
> Florists' picks
> Water picks
> Stickum
> Thin wire

1. Fasten the pinholder to the center of the compote with Stickum. Make sure that it is very firm since it must support the pineapple.
2. Impale the pineapple firmly on the pinholder.
3. Pull leaves from the top of the pineapple to make a pleasing curve (as if shaping an eyebrow).
4. Impale an apple on pins left vacant on each side of pineapple for additional foundation support.
5. Now, as if building with blocks and keeping triangular design in mind, pile other fruit on top of each other. To keep them from falling off, break a florists' pick in two, remove wire, and stick one end of the pick in the fruit on top and the other end into the fruit below. The reason for breaking the pick is that its entire length is not needed.
6. Use the curves of bananas and curved stems of pears to lead eye through design. Turn some of the apples with the stem end facing out for interest.
7. To complete symmetrical design, have a bunch of grapes hang over edge of compote at each side. You can make the bunches the shape and fullness you wish by pinching clusters from the back of the bunch where it may be too full and fastening these clusters where needed to fill out in front, by attaching them with thin wire. So that the bunches will fall gracefully from the edge of the compote, wire a florists' pick to the top stem and thrust the end of it into a firm fruit above. The bunch of grapes will then hang down from the edge of compote.
9. Insert pieces of foliage between fruit.

A fruit arrangement in shades of yellow, brown, and green. Note crescent design from top branch, through curved groove in estribo, to stem of farthest pear. This arrangement is perfect on a desk, mantel, or side table in a living room. *Photo by Roche. Arrangement by Katherine N. Cutler.*

Fruit arrangements are excellent to use as centerpieces on buffet tables. When the table is against a wall, you can use bold leaves for the background design. It's easy to coordinate color with the table setting. For an arrangement in shades of violet and red you might use canna or ti leaves with an eggplant, red and purple plums, red and purple grapes and pokeberry arranged on a jagged piece of gray flagstone. Or you could have an arrangement in shades of yellow and brown, using glycerined brown magnolia leaves (see page 78 for details) with a brown pineapple, bananas, brown-skinned onions, lemons, and yellow apples on a bamboo mat. Autumn berries are attractive used in combination with fruits and vegetables. Imagine brilliant orange fire-thorn berries used with orange-streaked green peppers, or turquoise berries with purple plums and grapes.

In our fuel-conserving environment, you could achieve a feeling of warmth by repeating the glow of the coals in an iron grate with an arrangement on a nearby table of polished dark red apples, purple plums, and red and purple grapes piled in an iron stove-top container. A further tie to the fire would be pieces of red and yellow coleus snipped from a house plant and inserted in the arrangement with hidden water picks.

With their bold forms and textures, fruit and vegetables are ideal for decoration in modern and contemporary houses. A fan of green bananas placed upright on a black base with accents of lemons and green-glass slag would be dramatic.

For an outdoor patio table you could have a "boat" made from a cocoanut spathe, palmetto cut in the shape of a sail, and a cargo of carefully arranged fruit.

Kitchen arrangements are fun, too. Instead of putting green fruit along a windowsill to ripen, did you ever think of making an arrangement with it? Some green tomatoes, a hard avocado, and some unripened plums, with the addition of a little parsley or mint (in water picks), could be an attractive arrangement to enjoy while you wait for it to ripen.

Arrangements of Dried and Pressed Flowers

Have you ever stood in your garden on a summer day, looking at a partly opened rose or an intensely blue delphinium, and thought, "Oh, if I could only save it until winter?" You *can* save it—by drying it. You can preserve that very rose and use it in an arrangement in January, when its parent bush is all covered with snow!

When thinking of dried arrangements, most people think only of those made with materials that dry naturally, like seedpods, pinecones, fungus, or weathered branches. These, in neutral shades of browns and grays, are lovely and very useful. But you can also have dried arrangements that are bursting with color and which evoke the feeling of spring and summer in the middle of dead winter. Best of all, they can be the very flowers that you have carefully tended in your garden. There are several ways to dry flowers, and the method depends on the type of flower you select.

Preserving Plants and Flowers

Hanging

One method of drying plants and flowers is by hanging. This is an easy process and works best with sturdy flowers that have strong stems such as cockscomb, goldenrod, lantern plant, honesty, euphorbia, yarrow, et cetera, or with a berried vine like bittersweet. Pick the flowers just before they reach their prime, except hydrangea, which should be left on the bush until a little past the height of bloom. Hydrangea will also dry well if they are left in their arrangement until all of the water evaporates.

How to Dry Plants by Hanging

1. Strip off any leaves.
2. Tie the flowers tightly in bunches so that as the stems dry and shrivel the bunch will hold together.
3. Hang most of them head down in a dry dark place such as a dark attic or a closet. Do not use a basement unless it is heated by a furnace because basements are apt to be damp. Also, it is very important that there be very little light since darkness preserves the color.
4. Instead of hanging all the bunches head down, stand some upright in a container and tie a weight to the cord that is binding them. The stems will bend as they dry, making delicate curves for your arrangements.
5. It will take from two to four weeks for the flowers to dry.

Drying plants by hanging

Drying
Mixtures

Another method of drying is to use a desiccant, or drying mixture. One such is silica gel, a granular substance sold in hardware stores and florist shops under names such as Flower-Dri. This looks like fine white sand dotted with bright blue granules and is an excellent and fast-drying medium for flowers. To use it, choose a container with a lid —a cookie or cake tin, or a coffee or nut can will work well. The larger containers will hold several flowers at one time, like daisies, zinnias, spray chrysanthemums, and others; the smaller ones are suitable for a single rose or dahlia.

To Dry Flowers with a Mixture

1. Put an inch or so of silica gel in the bottom of the container.
2. If the flower to be dried has a stiff stem, cut it an inch below the flower head. If the stem is weak, cut it completely off and thread a piece of fine wire up through the center of the flower head; bend it like a hairpin, push the end back through the flower, and wind it around the wire under the flower. (A longer wire stem can be attached to this later if desired.)
3. Place the flower on the silica gel. If the flower is flat like a daisy, place it head down. If it has many petals like a zinnia, place it head up. To dry a long spray such as delphinium, place notched pieces of cardboard vertically in box and place spray across notches.
4. Gently sift silica gel around and between the petals until the flower is covered.
5. Place the lid on the container and seal it with masking tape so that it is airtight. Mark the date on the lid.
6. You will have to experiment with the amount of time needed for the drying process as it depends on the thickness of the petals and their density. Four days to a week would be a general guide. If you uncover them and find the flowers are not completely dry, no harm is done. Leave them uncovered in the silica gel until you feel they are ready.

Using a Drying Mixture

False stems

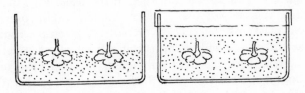

Flat flowers—heads down

More petals—heads up

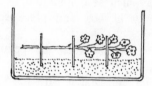

Long sprays—vertical

To remove the flowers: Tip the container and let the desiccant flow out slowly. Don't pull the flower out, but let it drop into your hand. If any residue remains on the flower, remove it gently with a watercolor brush. Reinforce the wire stem if necessary, and wrap it with green florists' tape. (If you do not plan to use the flowers right away, keep them in airtight plastic bags until you need them.)

You can use silica gel over and over. The blue granules give you a clue as to their effectiveness. When they turn pink, the maximum absorption has been reached. At that point, put the silica gel in a flat pan, and place the pan in a 250° oven until the granules turn blue again. Let it cool, and the silica gel is ready for more use.

Quick Drying

The recently popular microwave ovens make it easy to dry flowers very quickly. You use the silica gel in the usual way, but it is important that you do *not* use a metal container. Use ovenproof dishes (without a lid) of china, glass, or pottery. Place the container in the middle of the oven with a cup (again *not* metal) of water at the back of the oven. Turn the oven on. Again, you will have to experiment with the timing, but two and a half *minutes* is a guide. Wait until the desiccant has cooled before removing the container from the oven. This is a particularly successful method for fragile flowers like irises, daffodils, or lilies.

Drying
with
Sand

If silica gel is not available, you can use sand with satisfactory re-
sults. If you use beach sand, the salt content must be removed. To do
this, fill a large bucket or preserving kettle two thirds full of sand, and
add water to the brim. Stir the sand round and round and then pour
off the water. Repeat this process seven times. Then spread out the
sand in the sun, or put it in the oven to dry.

Instead of beach sand, you can buy the kind sold at a lumberyard
for children's sandboxes. This does not require the washing process but
should be sifted to remove any debris. Use sand in the same way you
use silica gel. It will take longer for the flowers to dry in sand—from
one to four weeks—but many people think that the flowers have a
more natural appearance since they are not excessively dehydrated.
Again, you must experiment, but the challenge of this is part of what
makes drying flowers such fun.

I have a favorite vase in my bedroom, and every summer I dry especially lovely single flowers from my garden to make a mixed bouquet I
can enjoy in winter. On a snowy day it brings back memories of those
sunny summer days which can seem so far away.

Pressing
Flowers

Another method of preserving flowers is to *press* them. These, of
course, will be flat, but they are lovely for making pictures, wall
plaques, place cards, bookmarks, and many other things. I keep some
old telephone books in my car, and when I see some flowers, grasses,
or ferns along the roadside that I think would press well, I gather them
and immediately put them between the pages of the telephone book
before they wilt. Some of the ferns I place in a curved position. Small
thin flowers like daisies, buttercups, violets, violas, and pansies press
well. And thin-leaved ferns like maidenhair are most satisfactory.

When I get home, I put a heavy sheet of blotting paper between the
pages of a heavy book and place the flowers and ferns carefully on the
blotting paper, making sure I keep the edges of the petals straight. I
then put another piece of blotting paper on top. Depending on how
much material you have, you can repeat this blotting-paper "sandwich"
every fifteen or so pages in the heavy book. Then put other heavy
books on top. The longer you keep the flowers in this way, without

peeking, the better the result will be. Three or four months is not too long a time.

Preserving
Foliage

You will need foliage for your dried arrangements, and there are three ways to preserve it. One is by pressing, as described above. This method works well for ferns, autumn leaves, and other leaves.

The second method of preserving foliage is to stand it in a solution of one third glycerin and two thirds warm water. (Glycerin can be bought in a drugstore.) The liquid should be three to five inches deep. With flat leaves like ivy or galax, immerse them in the solution and soak them flat.

The plant material must be fresh and mature. If it is too dry or too young, it will not preserve as successfully. *Note:* Do not set plant material in water before drying with glycerin solution. Crush or slit the ends of the branches so there is more area to absorb the solution. When tiny beads of moisture appear on the leaves, the foliage is ready to use.

This process of drying foliage usually takes from a few days to two weeks. The leaves will change color and be supple. You can use them over and over again. When they are not in use, store them in plastic bags and keep them in a cool place.

It is always fun to experiment with living material; and if there is some foliage that you think would be pretty, but isn't on any of the lists for glycerined material, why not try it anyway? You may come up with something unusual!

The third method of preserving foliage is again by *hanging.* Large single leaves like aspidistra, magnolia, canna, and rubber plant can be dried either hung upside down in a warm dry place or laid flat on a surface where air can circulate underneath. A cake or broiler rack works very well for this. Whichever way you do it, the edges of the leaves may curl and twist, but this makes the form more interesting.

To use these single dried leaves, fasten pieces of wire through the bottom long enough to double back and twist together. This makes a pliable sturdy stem and also makes it easy for you to place them for the best effect in your design.

To get beautiful curves with foliage like broom or podocarpus, cut it, allow it to get limp, and then tie it to curve in the shape you want— a crescent, S curve, circle, and so on. Put it in a dry place. When it is dry, untie it and it will stay in the shape you have formed.

**Drying Fruits
and Vegetables**

It is fun to experiment with drying fruits and vegetables. As always when working with living material, there is no guarantee of the result. Color and shape will change. Some will dry beautifully and others of the same variety will spoil and have to be discarded. (If they are soft but not rotten, don't throw them away as they will probably harden.) To dry fruits and vegetables, spread them on an open rack and leave them in a dry place for several weeks.

Among those that may be successful are artichokes, gourds, squash, string beans, and hot red peppers (wire the latter two in bunches before drying), Indian corn, okra, pomegranates, tangerines, and lemons.

Arranging Dried and Pressed Materials

You can arrange dried flowers and foliage just as you would fresh. In some ways it is easier to use dried materials because you can bend the wire "stems" in any direction, and stick them directly into a firm substance like Styrofoam, dry Oasis, or florists' clay. Make sure that it is well anchored. If you use a pinholder, you can put pieces of clay between the pins.

These colorful dried arrangements are particularly appropriate for houses with period furniture and decoration—Georgian, French, and Victorian. They were widely used in the early days of this country and have been made famous with the restoration of Williamsburg, where they are used in many of the buildings.

Arrangements of pods, cones, and dried branches, bold in form and brown, gray, or green in color, are suitable for contemporary decoration. Pods have a wonderful variety of interesting shapes. Yucca pods are like dark brown bells, milkweed is boat-shaped, and locust pods are long, narrow, and curved. When these are combined with linear material—manzanita branches, driftwood, and large dried leaves like canna, magnolia, and rubber plant—the effect is like a piece of bronze sculpture.

Wall panels and *plaques* using pods and cones make stunning decorations for rooms of contemporary design. To make one, first decide on the size and shape and choose a background to make it on. This can be a panel of wood or wall board, or a mat of burlap, monk's cloth, heavy linen, bamboo or straw. Next, plan the design as you would for a flower arrangement, with a definite pattern and center of interest. Assemble the different parts on a piece of paper until it is the way you want it. Then transfer the design to your chosen background piece by piece. If you are using wood, you can glue the pieces. With cloth, straw, or bamboo you can wire or sew the pieces on. (You can always back your cloth with wood if you want a very firm piece.)

It is fascinating to make pictures for a wall, or miniatures for a table with dried material. Always be on the lookout at antique shops or white elephant sales for small frames of shadowbox type or old-fashioned oval ones. If they are a little worse for wear, never mind. They will be less expensive and some paint and glue will restore them.

Cut a piece of thin wood or heavy cardboard to fit the frame, and cover it with velvet, grosgrain, silk, or cotton in a color you like for the background of your picture. Then, paying attention to scale, assemble a bouquet or nosegay of pressed flowers on the background. This is usually done in spray effect, with the stems making part of the picture. When you have the flowers placed where you want them, pick up each one and paint the back of it with glue, using a small watercolor brush. If the flowers are very small, it will help to handle them with tweezers. When the glue is dry, fit the background into the frame.

For a miniature, use a small frame like the oval gold-colored ones or an antique miniature or daguerreotype frame. Then follow the same procedure as for the picture except use tiny flowers and grasses, again being particular that each is in proper scale to the other and to the size of the frame.

Be creative with your dried arrangements; because they last so long, they can be used in many unusual ways. When I was decorating my youngest daughter's bedroom I needed a rather large lamp for a round table, and I didn't want to buy one if I could help it. I thought of making one out of a glass apothecary jar. Inside the jar I put a miniature Victorian vase filled with a bouquet of tiny old-fashioned flowers—dried lilies of the valley, forget-me-nots, violets, miniature roses, statice, and field grasses. I made as much of the arrangement as would slide through the opening at the top of the jar. Then I put some Stickum on the bottom of the vase and gently lowered it into the jar, pressing it down firmly so that the Stickum would adhere to the bottom of the jar. Then with tweezers I finished the arrangement. My husband bored a hole in the stopper of the jar to hold the electric fixture, and I bought a plain white shade. By featuring the dried bouquet, I had a charming and rather unusual lamp that was unbelievably inexpensive.

Another idea comes from one of my friends who inherited a lovely old silver watch that opened in three panels. She covered the middle panel with velvet and glued a spray of tiny dried flowers to it. This she uses as a most intriguing ornament on the bedside table in her guest room.

Perhaps dried material will be the answer to a decorating problem for you!

Suggested Plant Material for Dried Arrangements and Wall Plaques

For Line	*Seedpods*	*Other Material*
Broom	Baptisia	Acorns
Canna Leaves	Cotton	Artichokes
Castor Bean Leaves	Iris	Cattails
Date Palm Sprays	Lily	Cocoanut Calyxes
Dried Fern	Locust	Dock
Driftwood	Lotus	Dried Mullein Heads
Galax Leaves	Magnolia	Dried Okra
Magnolia Leaves	Mallow	Embryo Palm
Manzanita Branches	Okra	Fungi
Palmetto	Paulownia	Gourds
Palm Spathe	Thistle	Hot Red Peppers
Rubber Plant	Trumpet Vine	Indian Corn
Leaves		Lemon
Sea Grape Leaves		Lichens
Sea Oats		Lime
Wisteria Vine		Nuts
		Okra
		Pomegranate
		Pinecones
		(many varieties)
		Squash
		String Beans
		Sweet Gum Balls
		Tangerine
		Wood Rose

Flowers and Berries to Dry by Hanging

Pink, Red, and Rose	*Yellow and Orange*	*Blue, Lavender, and Purple*	*White and Gray*
Astilbe	Bittersweet	Astilbe	Artemisia
Bamboo	Chinese	Bachelor's	Astilbe
California	Lantern	Button	Baby's Breath
Pepper	Cockscomb	Globe	Bayberry
Clover	Goldenrod	Amarinth	Desert Holly
Cockscomb	Strawflower	Heather	Honesty
Heather		Hydrangea	Pussy Willow
Hydrangea		Joe-Pye-Weed	Queen Anne's
Rose Hips		Statice	Lace
Scarlet Sage		Thistle	Snow-on-the-
Statice			Mountain
Strawflower			

Foliage to Dry with Glycerin Solution

Bayberry
Beech
Dogwood
Galax
Ivy
Laurel
Leucothoë
Magnolia
Maple (Japanese)
Rhododendron
Viburnum

Flowers to Dry in Sand or Silica Gel

Aster
Anemone
Azalea
Bells of Ireland
Buttercup
Calendula
Clematis
Carnation
Dahlia
Delphinium
Daisy
Gerbera
Lily
Marigold
Narcissus
Queen Anne's Lace
Rose
Syringa
Snapdragon
Stock
Tulip
Violet
Zinnia

Wildflower Arrangements

For many of us the word *wildflower* is nostalgic. We remember the thrill, when we were children, of finding the first spring violets, of seeing a pink carpet of spring beauties in the woods or masses of bluebells by a winding river. Although wildflowers have botanical names, the ones by which we know them best are the affectionate, descriptive ones they were given long ago by people who loved them. Just to say "Jack-in-the-pulpit," "butter-and-eggs," or "buttercup" brings the picture of a flower to mind.

Nature has been lavish with these flowers. No cultivated garden can compete with the sheer abundance of flowers found in fields white with daisies, yellow with mustard and buttercups, red with clover, or pink and purple with Joe-Pye-weed and wild asters. Because of their abundance, we are apt to think of them as commonplace and ignore the very real beauty they have.

Dainty Queen Anne's lace, looking like a magnified snowflake, is so taken for granted that it often goes unnoticed, although its cultivated cousin, blue lace flower, is a big seller in florist shops. White field daisies make as cheerful a bouquet in summer as hot house marguerites do in winter. Wild catbrier grows in as intriguing curves as a carefully nurtured clematis vine. Goldenrod, whose golden plumes line roadsides in the fall and turn fields into waving seas of gold, is hybridized in England and prized as a garden flower. Goldenrod, incidentally, has been maligned for years because many think its pollen causes hay fever. It is interesting to know that a recent study claims the pollen of goldenrod is too heavy to blow very far on autumn winds and the other flowers and grasses blooming at the same time are really the hay fever culprits.

One of the things that is most fun to do in spring, summer, and fall is to combine a picnic with a pilgrimage to gather wildflowers. Before you go on one, though, there are several important things to consider. First of all, all fields and woods belong to *someone,* and before you open your picnic baskets and gather flowers, you should find the

Delicate Queen Anne's lace, one of our best-loved wildflowers is used here in an antique container to make a beautiful arrangement. *Photo by Roche. Arrangement by Mary Alice Roche.*

owner, if possible, and ask permission. Second, some of our most beautiful wildflowers are becoming rare almost to the point of extinction, and these must be conserved. Know the wildflowers that are on conservation lists in your state and *don't pick them*. The Wildflower Preservation Society in Washington, D.C., publishes a comprehensive list and you can write for this. Also, a most important precaution is to become familiar with poisonous plants like poison ivy, poison oak, and poison sumac so that you can keep your distance from them, and your picnic won't end up in misery. And last, leave the woods in the same condition in which you found them!

Recently this was dramatically brought home to some people who live in a neighboring town. They had a gay picnic in some woods by a waterfall, unknowingly observed by the owner of the property. Although they hadn't asked his permission, he didn't mind that they picked bouquets of wildflowers, but he did mind that when they left the area was littered with papers, bottles, banana peels, and other debris. He took the number of their license plate, found out where they lived, and the following Sunday drove to their home on a fashionable suburban street. As the owners, entertaining guests on the terrace watched aghast, the man proceeded to dump trash on the manicured lawn. When they remonstrated, he said, "I am just returning the things you left on my property last week."

Handling Fresh-picked Wildflowers

Because you are apt to pick wildflowers at a distance from home, it is wise to take a container of water with you. Put a pail in the back of the car or carry a jar of water in your flower basket. If you don't want to carry water, take some plastic bags with a little water in the bottom of them, put in the flowers, and close the top so that there will be humidity inside. If they are wilted when you get home, don't forget the hot-water treatment recommended in the section on Conditioning.

Wildflowers seem to like an extra drink, so allow a little more time for them to harden than for other flowers. Some of the flowers are more fragile than others. By putting them in water immediately and keeping them in water overnight, I have had good luck with some that are supposed to wilt quickly, like spring beauties, wild geraniums, and primroses.

It is fun to walk along a country road and get flowers for a mixed bouquet. A flower-arranging friend, visiting me in New Jersey from California, said, "I think I'll take a walk and see what I can find here

A typical fall wildflower arrangement of goldenrod, wild aster, berries, and fall foliage.

for an arrangement." In twenty minutes she was back with a lovely fall bouquet of wild asters, goldenrod, boneset, Joe-Pye-weed, purple viburnum berries, red viburnum foliage, and purple blackberry vine. Arranged in a brass wood bucket it was much admired, and more than one person said, "And you really found all this along the roadside?"

You would think that wildflowers at the seashore would be very rugged and sturdy to be able to stand the high winds and salt spray—and I guess they are—but in appearance they are deceptively fragile-looking and among the most beautiful. One of the first to appear is the beach plum—a drift of dainty white flowers over the dunes. Then follow beach peas, like miniature sweet peas with gray-green vines and tendrils. There are delicate pink wild roses, fragile blue irises, and exquisite pink, red, and white mallows—cousins of the tropical hibiscus.

Save-a-Plant

There is one time when it is permissible to gather wildflowers that are on the *rare* list. This is when you know the property where they are growing is about to be cleared for developing or building. In fact, the most satisfactory thing to do, if you can, is to dig up the whole plant and plant it at home rather than have it fall victim to a bulldozer. If there is a corner in your garden that is shady or wooded and the soil is acid, you can rescue wild azalea, trillium, bloodroot, and wild columbine, to name a few.

At the entrance to the town where we live at the seashore, there is a large pond. One of the main projects of our garden club is to rescue plants that are native to the area and plant them on the shores of the pond. This is rapidly developing into a little natural park, and at the rate building has gone in the last few years if it were not for this rescuing project, some of the native plants would have entirely disappeared from the area.

Because wildflowers and trees such as dogwood are so attractive, many people grow them in their gardens, and although material on conservation lists is forbidden in flower shows, exceptions are being made for exhibits containing such material if accompanied by a card stating, "grown by exhibitor."

There is great satisfaction in gathering wildflowers, because most of us, whether we admit it or not, love getting "something for nothing." However, if you want wild plants for your garden that are on rare or conservation lists, you can buy them from excellent nurseries that specialize in wild plants.

Below is a list of some of the more familiar wildflowers:

Save	*Pick Discriminately*	*Pick Freely*
Bittersweet	Anemone	Black-eyed Susan
Bluebells	Bellflower	Boneset
Cardinal Flower	Bloodroot	Bouncing Bet
Columbine	Blue-eyed Grass	Bush Clover

Save	*Pick Discriminately*	*Pick Freely*
Dogwood	Blue Flag	Butter-and-Eggs
Gentian	Bluets	Buttercup
Ginseng	Bush Honeysuckle	Clover
Ground Pine	Butterfly Weed	Daisy
Hepatica	Dogtooth Violet	Dandelion
Holly	Dutchman's Breeches	Day Lily
Lady's Slipper	Huckleberry	Goldenrod
Maidenhair Fern	Marsh Marigold	Jewel Weed
Mountain Laurel	Mayapple	Joe-Pye-Weed
Orchids	Mistletoe	Mallow
Partridgeberry	Shadbush	Milkweed
Pipsissewa	Sheep Laurel	Morning Glory
Pitcher Plant	Spring Beauty	Mullein
Prince's Pine	Star-of-Bethlehem	Mustard
Rhododendron	Tulip Tree	Pickerelweed
Solomon's Seal	Turtlehead	Pokeweed
Trailing Arbutus	Violet	Queen Anne's
Trillium	Water Lily	Lace
Walking Fern	Wild Ageratum	Skunk Cabbage
	Wild Geranium	Sunflower
	Wild Rose	Sweet Clover
	Wintergreen	Tansy
		Thistle
		Wild Aster
		Yarrow

Arranging
with House Plants

There are times when it is practical to use a house plant for decorative arrangements rather than cut flowers. At certain times of the year, flowers are scarce and expensive in many parts of the country. Or there may be an occasion when you have no time to plan and gather flowers for a flower arrangement. Or you may simply want to use your house plants in a new way—adding beauty to your home and a new usefulness to your plants.

**Containers
Are the
Key**

By choosing a container that is imaginative you can make a single ordinary plant a most decorative feature. Such a container might be a large shell, natural or ceramic, a kettle, a soup tureen, or a pretty cachepot or antique compote. One of the most available and easiest to grow house plants—*Philodendron cordatum*—is shown here planted in a brass teakettle and placed on a teakwood stand. The choice of container and stand transforms a rather commonplace plant into a distinctive decorative feature. The nice part is that it will continue to be lovely with very little care—just some water, a little food, and an occasional syringing of the leaves to keep them free of dust and insects.

Potted plants are a godsend to use on a dining-room table in winter, when it is a problem to find flowers for a centerpiece. Here again, it is important to choose distinctive containers. You will also have to choose plants that will grow without direct sunlight. Holly fern is one of these. I always associate holly fern with a mad dog! When I was a

This is a good example of the imaginative use of a container not originally designed for plants. Here philodendron planted in a brass kettle placed on a small stand makes an unusual windowsill decoration. *Photo by Roche.*

child, my four-year-old sister was bitten by a mad dog. For twenty-three days she had to be taken from our small town to New York, fifty miles away, for Pasteur treatment. In those days this aroused a great deal of interest and sympathy; she was showered with presents and even the rest of the family got some. My mother was given four charming, squat, silver-monogrammed flowerpots and from that time on these pots, filled with holly fern through most of my growing years, formed the centerpiece for our dining table in the winter months.

One woman I know, whose house is very formal, uses a beautiful centerpiece when she gives a dinner party in the winter. She happens to grow many varieties of African violets under artificial light in her basement. At the time of a party, she fills a handsome deep Sheffield basket with pots of violet—deep purple in the middle and others, ranging from the blue and lavender shades to rose and pink, on the outside. Placed between silver candelabra this is a fascinating centerpiece.

There are wall brackets sold commercially that when filled with plants are stunning on the plain walls of contemporary or Spanish-type houses. They are usually made of wrought iron in the shape of vines and leaves, with metal circles attached to hold pots. I know of a house where the only decoration in a rather small dining room with plain walls is one of these fixtures sprawling over one wall. The pots, holding trailing philodendron, are of glazed yellow pottery the color of the dining-room chairs. The effect is unusual, refreshing, and gay.

Hanging Baskets

A hanging basket of growing plants arranged for artistic effect makes a conversation piece for a patio, porch, or terrace. You should be sure in planning such a basket that the plants you select will survive under the same growing conditions. To make a hanging basket:

1. Buy a wire basket or an openwork straw one.
2. Line it with moss placed with the green side out, or line it with sphagnum moss.
3. Fill it to within an inch or two of the top with good garden soil mixed with some peat moss.
4. Put the unpotted plants directly in the soil, arranging them for color and effect. Be sure to press the soil firmly around the roots.

Check the soil daily to see if it is dry. If it is, water it thoroughly so that it gets to the roots. Plants that are exposed to wind need watering more frequently than sheltered ones.

Plants that adapt well to hanging baskets are:

Begonia (many varieties)	Geranium	Pothos
	Ivy Geranium	Spider Plant
Coleus	Piggyback Plant	Swedish Ivy
Ferns	Philodendron	Tradescantia
Fuchsia		Variegated Ivy

Cutting Garden

Sometimes in a house there will be a windowsill that is ideal for growing plants in a room that doesn't need decoration. It might be in a utility room, a pantry, or a garage. These are wonderful places to have a miniature cutting garden—a place where you can grow house plants which you can cut from. Some leaves of *Syngonium* or angel-wing or rex begonia may be just what you need for a focal point, or on the night of a dressy dinner party you can cut leaves of rose geranium to float in the finger bowls.

Special Care for House Plants

House plants need much the same care that we do. They must have food, water, and fresh air. They need to be bathed and groomed, and they seem to respond to affectionate care. Care should be taken not to overwater house plants. Believe it or not, more plants die from overwatering than underwatering. A good way to tell whether a plant needs to be watered is to feel the soil at the top of the pot. If it feels dry to your fingertips, it needs water. Fill the space from the top of the soil to the rim on the pot with water and let it seep in; repeat until no more water is absorbed and air bubbles have stopped rising.

Spray the foliage of plants (except African violets) with water. This creates more humidity, improves their appearance, helps them breathe by keeping them free of dust. It also helps to keep them pest-free.

Feed plants by following the directions on the plant food sold at a florist or variety store, and establish a regular feeding pattern. Just as you wouldn't give your children a large dose of vitamins one week, and then skip giving them any for several weeks, it isn't good to feed plants so that they take a big spurt and then limp along without food for a while. Feed plants when soil is moist because it is easier for the food to be distributed evenly than when soil is dry.

You can take many foliage house plants out of the pots and use them for arrangements as though they were cut flowers. The roots continue to grow in water, or, if you are using single leaves, many will root themselves. Use a nontransparent container so the roots won't show. Add a piece of charcoal to the water to keep it from developing a sour smell. Select the combination you want, according to color, texture, and form. You might use Chinese evergreen, sansevieria, or dracaena for height, with trailing vines of pothos, ivy, or tradescantia. Some of the oddly shaped philodendron, rex begonia, or *Syngonium* would make a distinctive center of interest.

Sometimes when a house plant such as a geranium has grown thin and leggy, it is best to cut it drastically. Then you can choose a distinctive container and make an arrangement using the cut material.

Here is a list of plants suitable for decoration and the locations in which they grow best.

South Window (*Most Light*)	East or West Window (*Good Light*)	North Window or Completely Indoors (*Least Light*)
Abutilon	Abutilon	Aspidistra
Anthurium	African Violet	Baby's Tears
Azalea	Begonia	Boston Fern
Cactus	Caladium	Chinese Evergreen
Crown of Thorns	Christmas Cactus	Cyperus
Cyclamen	Chrysanthemum	Dieffenbachia
Gardenia	Coleus	English Ivy
Geranium	Dracaena	Fatshedera
Hibiscus	Echeveria	Fittonia
Jade Plant	Fuchsia	Grape Ivy
Jerusalem Cherry	Gloxinia	Holly Fern
Morning Glory	Maidenhair Fern	Kangeroo Vine
Otaheite Orange	Maranta	Monstera
Poinsettia	Mimosa Pudica	Nephthytis
Primrose	Peperomia	Norfolk Island Pine
Shrimp Plant	Piggyback Plant	Pandanus
Thunbergia	Podocarpus	Philodendron
	Spider Plant	Pothos
	Succulents	Ribbon Fern
	Thunbergia	Sansevieria
		Schefflera
		Spathyphyllum
		Syngonium
		Tradescantia

Miniature Arrangements

One of the most fascinating types of arrangements is the small, or miniature, arrangement. Miniatures range in size from less than an inch to 8″ overall. It is probably the most fun of all to create, but presents the biggest challenge in scale and proportion.

To adhere to the guiding principle that an arrangement should be 1½ times the height of the container, the container for an arrangement 8″ overall should not be *over* 3″ tall, but it could be any size *under* that down to the most minuscule. For instance, both a 3″ high pitcher and a pitcher from a dollhouse tea set less than an inch high would qualify as a container for a miniature arrangement. The problem would be to see that the plant material is in proper scale to the container.

A guide for proper scaling is that the largest flower should not be over one third the size of the container. That is, for the 3″ pitcher the largest flower used should not be more than 1″ in diameter. As the size of the container diminishes so does the relative size of the largest flower. In a 3″ pitcher, the size of small flowers like dwarf marigolds or zinnias, buttercups or violets would be appropriate. However, their natural foliage might be too large in scale, so other smaller greens should be substituted.

While these arrangements are very attractive, it is in the really small ones where the fun begins because the smaller the container the more imagination you must use in choosing plant material. Twigs and sturdy vine tendrils can simulate the bare branches used in conventional large arrangements—a tiny side shoot of blue sage or a snip of vitex; a stalk of delphinium or a minute piece of heather; a stalk of stock or a floret of statice; a carnation or a single kalenchoe blossom; a camellia or a coral bell; a tulip, a single flower of candytuft, or a daisy. Snippets of parsley or boxwood provide foliage in proper scale.

The best test of whether a miniature arrangement is in proper scale is that, when photographed, one would not be able to tell whether it was a miniature or a very large arrangement unless the scale was shown by some object such as a thimble photographed alongside it.

Some suggestions for miniature fruit arrangements that really fool the eye: privet berries simulating hothouse black grapes; tiny clusters of andromeda buds simulating green grapes; holly berries simulating apples; bittersweet berries simulating oranges; and seeds simulating nuts.

Base

Just as a large arrangement is often made more important by using a base, so is a miniature one. Here again you must consider proper scale of base to container. For instance, suppose you use a lipstick tube as the container for the miniature of a tall arrangement. A button, used as a base with the convex side up, would add distinction.

Mechanical Aids

There are special mechanics for miniature arrangements. A tiny piece of Oasis is good since it not only holds the tiny stems but holds water for a comparatively long time. Because some of the stems are so tiny, it may be necessary to make holes in the Oasis for them with a toothpick and then insert the stems with tweezers. You can buy very small pinholders and, for a flat container, fasten the pinholder in a tube cap or lid to make a tiny cup pinholder. For miniature dried arrangements you can fill a bottle cap with clay.

A list of suggested plant material, containers, and bases for miniature arrangements follows:

Plant Material	*Containers*	*Bases*
Acacia	Doll china	Buttons
Acacia Foliage	Lids	Copper pennies
African Violet	Liquor glasses	Driftwood
Alyssum	Minute shells	Mirrors
Baby's Breath	Perfume bottles	Sea glass
Begonia	Pill bottles	Slate
Bittersweet	Open salts	Wood chips
Blue Sage	Stamp boxes	
Boxwood	Thimbles	
Candytuft	Tiny baskets	

Plant Material	*Containers*
Cedar Berries	Toothpick holders
Coralbell	Top of individual
Feverfew	salts
Fire Thorn Berries	
Forget-me-not	
Grape Hyacinth	
Gypsophila	
Heather	
Holly Berries	
Ilex	
Kalanchoe	
Lily of the Valley	
Miniature Ivy	
Miniature Rose	
Parsley	
Pepper Berries	
Privet Berries	
Salvia	
Statice	
Vine Tendrils	
Vitex	

Miniature arrangements should be seen at close range where their intricacies can be studied. They make wonderful gifts for invalids' trays and bedside tables. They can be unusual favors for a party table. For people who collect miniature furniture, a bouquet in proper scale to fit on a tiny table or desk is a highly prized acquisition. One woman I know completely decorated a friend's miniature living room for Christmas as her present. She made miniature garlands for the mantel, a miniature Della Robbia wreath for over the fireplace, and a mass arrangement of greens and minute red berries in a tiny brass container for the top of a little chest of drawers.

Dried material in miniature has many uses. You can make place cards (as described in the section on Thanksgiving) and Christmas cards. Miniature dried arrangements in lovely antique miniature or daguerreotype frames are exquisite decorative accessories.

It is fun, too, to make miniature fruit and vegetable arrangements. For a container, you could use a footed salt cellar that would serve as a miniature compote; and use rose hips for apples, Brussels sprouts for cabbages, privet berries for grapes, green acorns minus shell for avocados, euonymous berries for tomatoes, pyrocantha berries for persimmons, and bittersweet berries for oranges. Wouldn't such an arrangement be just the thing for an invalid's tray at Thanksgiving?

Budget Arrangements

The other day a young bride said to me, "I would love to have fresh flowers in my home, but I live in a city apartment and have to buy them and they seem like such a luxury item. Besides, when I do go to a florist, I hesitate to buy one of this and one of that and yet I like a mixture." My friend suffers from two common misconceptions. First, don't hesitate to go into a shop and plan a mixed bouquet on the spot. Also, my young friend was wrong in thinking that fresh flowers are a luxury. Perhaps she's right if she is thinking of buying long-stemmed roses; or if she is lured by the low price into buying flowers from a street vendor. The latter may look fresh but will probably wilt overnight.

Economical Flowers

If you go to a reliable florist, and learn which flowers give the greatest value for your money, and use imagination in your combination of flowers and container, it is possible to have fresh flowers without making too big a hole in the weekly housekeeping budget. Look for varieties that grow in sprays. Each stalk has several branches and on them are flowers in all stages of development, from buds to full blown. This is true of *spray chrysanthemums, freesias, yellow daisies, marguerites,* and miniature *carnations.* You can snip off the fully opened flowers to use as a focal point, the budded stems for line, and the partially opened ones for transition between.

Heather is another economical flower. It grows with sprays tapering from a full cluster at the bottom to a thin end at the top. You can have a mass bouquet of heather without the addition of other flowers. It lasts a long time, and when it is dry it is still lovely to add to a dried bouquet.

A few sprays of *yellow acacia* will form a beautiful line arrangement, and it too is lovely when it dries.

As you watch it gradually open, a single perfect *rosebud* in a bud vase on a coffee table can give as much pleasure as a whole bowlful of flowers.

A piece of driftwood, leaves from a house plant, and three large chrysanthemums make an inexpensive arrangement suitable for a large space. *Photo by Denby Versfeld Associates. Arrangement by Katherine N. Cutler.*

Less
Is
More

For a large space in a living room, such as the top of a piano or a large wall area, think of using three flowers instead of a dozen. You can get the bold, sweeping lines you need with foliage or bare branches, and then use three large flowers for accent. If you have collected branches and dried vines of interesting shape, this is the time to bring them out. Foliage such as broom or podocarpus can be bent, as described in the section on Foliage Arrangements, and used with three flowers like tulips, dahlias, or carnations that follow the curve, or that are grouped at different levels at the base. Vary the form of a tulip and make it look like a large, round, open flower by gently turning back the petals with your fingertips. If you do it carefully, it doesn't injure the blossom and it creates an interesting form because it shows the center of the flower. The foliage will last several weeks and you can make it seem completely different by varying the color and form of the flower accent.

Huckleberry, which a florist often includes free of charge with a flower purchase, grows flat and, for this reason, is well suited to mantel arrangements. You might make twin arrangements in matching containers with a few flowers as an accent.

If you have an interesting candelabrum, you can make it your centerpiece for a party table. Take out the center candle, and instead fasten a soaked piece of Oasis to the opening with wire. Make a nosegay by taking a few small flowers and combining them with some ivy or other foliage stuck in Oasis. This will make the candelabrum a really impressive centerpiece.

Fruit fits well into budget arrangements. It serves a double purpose. One January day I stopped in to see a young neighbor and found her preparing for a company dinner. "What can I do for a centerpiece?" she said. "I forgot about flowers, and I have only enough money left in my budget this week for food." I looked around and saw a pewter scale on her sideboard. "Don't you have a pewter compote?" I asked. She nodded affirmatively. I said, "Why not get some red apples and some grapes, and pick some of that green euonymous outside? Make arrangements of apples and grapes in the scale for the sideboard, and in the compote for the table. After your dinner party you can use them for applesauce and Waldorf salad. That way you can make your food money double for your flower money." We tried it and her dinner party was a success.

Arrangements Using Artificial Flowers

There was a time when a flower arranger would have thrown up her hands in horror and said, "Heavens, no!" if asked whether she ever used artificial flowers in an arrangement. In recent years, though, the art of making artificial flowers has been so perfected that many of them are exquisite and look so real that you have to touch them to know they're not. Although there are a few diehards, most experts admit that there is a place for artificial flowers. I was secretly amused not long ago when a lecturer, who was using some to make a point in her demonstration, couldn't bring herself to say "artificial flowers" and referred to them as "permanent material."

No matter how well it is made, however, an artificial flower can't equal a real one. The principal reason is that the real flower is living and breathing. With an artificial one there is no slight movement of a petal or leaf. It is completely static. When you see a bouquet of artistically arranged artificial flowers in a room, you may think, "That certainly looks real." But when you stay in the room and look at it for a while, you become conscious of that static difference.

I am thinking of one arrangement in particular. When I first saw it in the house of a friend, I thought, "How lovely!" Now, after seeing it in the same place for two years, looking exactly the same, I think, "How boring." A big argument against using artificial arrangements is that people tend to regard them as they do pictures on a wall—once placed, they are left there indefinitely. This is fine for an art form in which there is always something new to see, but with a flower arrangement, much of the charm comes from its living quality, and I think subconsciously we resent it when it is static.

For this reason, if you want to use artificial flowers, why not have a collection of the ones you prefer and bring different ones out, from time to time, to use along with real foliage? In this way you get the color and form of the flowers, but the arrangement isn't static. For instance, you can buy very real-looking rhododendron blossoms. Rhododendron foliage is available most of the year, but the blossoms last only a short time. So why not make an arrangement of the real foliage and wire on the artificial blossoms (only don't leave the arrangement in place until people are tired of it). It is difficult in some spots to have geraniums bloom in the winter, but the foliage grows luxuriantly. Try wiring a few artificial geranium blossoms to the leafy plants.

You can also use this live-and-artificial combination with fruit. As anyone who likes to do fruit arrangements knows, you are limited by seasonable material. The very thing you need most to accent the arrangement is not available in the market. You can keep an assortment of quite real-looking artificial fruit on hand, and add a bunch of purple grapes, a pomegranate, a persimmon, or a peach to the arrangement, and no one will be the wiser. (I am not speaking of flower shows, of course.)

There are some instances where artificial material can be a godsend. One of my friends found this out when she bought a summer house with a two-storied living room. At one end is a massive stone fireplace with a chimneypiece reaching to the ceiling. High above the mantel is a niche set into the stone. She was at her wits' end to know what to do with the niche until she thought of artificial plants. She bought a long, narrow container to fit the opening and filled it with artificial sansevieria, philodendron, bells of Ireland, and other greens. The effect is natural and stunning, and it would be impossible to use real plants in this case. There isn't enough light in the niche for them to grow properly, and you would need to use a ladder to water them.

Most people have a definite color scheme for their dining rooms, carried through wallpaper, draperies, tablecloths, and china. Sometimes there aren't any flowers available for a table centerpiece in this color scheme. This is another time when it is convenient to have artificial flowers of the proper size and color on hand.

Another place where artificial flowers could easily be the answer is a doctor's office or waiting room. These are busy places and there is usually no time for rearranging bouquets or caring for plants. People may be nervous and apprehensive in such a room and would much rather look at a gay bouquet of artificial flowers than a drooping house plant. Besides, different people are coming and going and aren't there long enough for the arrangement to become boring.

Artificial material is also fun for "tongue in cheek" decorating. I saw a clever use of it the other day in a guest apartment over a garage. The enclosed stairway leading up to it has open risers. So that mosquitoes can't get into the openings from the garage space, the openings are screened. The decorator conceived the idea of putting artificial ivy between the screening. With the treads of the stairs painted white you now have the impression of climbing up white stairs set into a bank of ivy.

Yes—there is a place for artificial material—but *do* use fresh when possible!

Period
Arrangements

Throughout the ages, flower arrangements have been influenced by the life style, culture, and religion of different periods in time. Therefore, we have come to speak of them as Period Arrangements. Each period has characteristics of its own. Since many of them are reflected in our homes today, it is interesting to list some of them briefly:

Ancient Egyptian (2800 B.C.–A.D. 28): Characterized by stylized designs with great clarity. Tall narrow vases, urns, and chalice cups were used as containers.

Chinese (A.D. 960): Extreme restraint; reverence of nature.

Dutch and Flemish (seventeenth and eighteenth centuries): Full mass arrangements, showing great horticultural interest of the times by including many varieties of flowers in one arrangement. Accessories included birds' nests, fruit, butterflies, and decanters of wine.

French (eighteenth century): Loose, airy, asymmetrical mass bouquets in pastel colors of more elegant flowers. Exquisite urns, epergnes, and vases of porcelain, alabaster, and marble were used as containers.

Georgian (eighteenth and nineteenth centuries): Dignified symmetrical mass arrangements suitable for stately homes of England. Containers were of fine pottery and silver.

Early American (seventeenth century): Simple mixed bouquets of simple garden and field flowers. Containers were often a utensil—iron pot, salt box, bottles, and baskets.

Colonial American (eighteenth century): This covers the period when wealthy settlers came to the Williamsburg area, bringing with them plants from England and Europe. Dried flowers came into favor, and many bouquets were composed of them. After the American Revolution, French influence was felt. There were mass arrangements in harmonious color schemes. Containers of porcelain, glass, and silver were formal in shape.

Victorian (nineteenth and early twentieth centuries): Crowded mass arrangements containing garden and field flowers, herbs and grasses were popular. Ornate, heavily decorated vases, flaring from the base in a fan shape, were characteristic, as were those of milk glass, satin and pressed glass, and Parian ware.

While it is only in a flower show schedule that an authentic period arrangement is required, it is easy to see how arrangements influenced by these periods are suitable for houses in this country; the houses can also be categorized according to some period of the country's development—Early American, Southern Colonial, Georgian, Dutch, Victorian, Spanish, and Contemporary. Under Contemporary there are really two classes—the houses sometimes called Modern, a development of this century using clean-cut lines and great expanses of glass, and the houses that are of no particular period but have features of several and are furnished with a comfortable accumulation of old and new belongings.

We know that from the time the first settlers came, people had gardens and decorated their houses with flowers. The styles in which they arranged them, the types of flowers, and the containers they used were governed by the location and manner in which they lived.

The early New Englanders were too busy struggling to grow food in the rocky soil to have flower gardens. The few flowers they did grow by their doorsteps or in windows were the result of seeds and slips which they brought with them—bright sturdy flowers like geraniums and marigolds. How they must have rejoiced in the wealth of wildflowers and shrubs in the New England woods, and with what delight they must have filled their utilitarian containers—iron pots, jugs, wooden kegs, and pewter bowls.

It was quite different, on the other hand, for the settlers in the southern colonies. These were the wealthy traders who had slaves to cultivate flowers as well as cotton. Because of the temperate climate, plants grew easily and, in addition to the native ones, plants were imported from abroad. Also imported were containers of silver, porcelain, and rare china. These were usually in the shape of a widemouthed bowl or a classic urn and were well suited to the elegant mass bouquets of roses, lilies, carnations, tulips, and stock that decorated rooms filled with beautiful furniture and fabrics. Many of these bouquets were inspired from Georgian England.

At this time, too, many things were imported from France. Flower containers from France were slender vases of porcelain or delicately carved urns of alabaster. Bouquets, though still of mass type, were delicate, airy, and feathery. Flowers were of pastel colors to go with the dainty furniture and pale silk fabrics.

Wealthy Dutch settlers in the Middle Atlantic states brought with them sturdier, but no less beautiful, containers, and their arrangements reflected the Flemish—mass bouquets with an abundance of material in vivid colors.

In the Victorian period, furniture was heavy and dark. Fabrics were thick and richly colored and rooms were filled to bursting with ornaments. Many new flowers were introduced because of expanding world trade, and the mass arrangements of the period reflected the "busyness" of the general decor. Not only were many varieties of cultivated flowers used, but they were also combined with wildflowers, herbs, and grasses. Containers were decorated with paintings or raised gold designs or a combination of both. They were also made of many kinds of glass—Sandwich, Bristol, milk, and satin. The typical Victorian container was flat and fan-shaped.

The Spanish settlers of the Southwest brought heavy carved furniture and colorful utensils—tall pottery jars, copper baking pans, copper milk jugs, and wrought-iron trays. These made perfect containers in scale and color for their tropical flowers—hibiscus, bougainvillea, camellias, calla lilies, and bird-of-paradise.

Strangely enough, for the Modern or Contemporary house, typical of this century, ancient Egyptian arrangements look very good. In these houses with their large areas of bare wall and floor-to-ceiling expanses of glass, the clean-cut lines and dramatic, stylized designs of ancient Egypt seem very much at home.

In the present day we make use of arrangements of all periods. We are not limited to being absolutely authentic in relating type of house with the proper period. An eighteenth-century arrangement, not too elegant in appointments, could be perfectly at home in an Early American house—a colonial American arrangement would look fine in a Dutch colonial home. However, a fussy Victorian arrangement *would* look out of place in a modern house with wide expanses of wood and glass. The trick is to consider the type of house you live in, its furnishings and decor, use periods as a guide, and be influenced accordingly when you choose flowers and containers.

Contemporary and Abstract Arrangements

So far, the flower arrangements we have discussed have been along traditional lines—principles that have survived for centuries. However, today there is a tendency to abandon the conventional and try something new, and for many people this is true in flower arrangement. Contemporary and abstract arrangements give great scope for creativity. There is more freedom to experiment—an acceptance of new attitudes and ideas. However, successful modern or abstract arranging has had a strong foundation in traditional design.

Modern arrangements are appropriate for contemporary architecture. They are bold in line, shape, and color, with a clean-cut design. Yet the components may be arranged in the traditional way—carrying the eye to and from a central point of radiation. Today's arranger may ask, "While keeping the basic good points of a traditional arrangement, what can I do to give it a new look?" The key might simply be an unusual container of modern design or one that is bold in color or texture; or try an unusual color combination or an unconventional accessory. Modern arrangements have a strong line, a distinct use of space in the design, and restraint in the quantity of material.

Perhaps I can best illustrate how to create a modern arrangement by describing one that I saw made, step by step, by an exhibitor for an International Flower Show given here. (It later won top awards.)

With nothing yet decided but the title of her class (Midnight Mushroom) and the space to be filled (a height of ten feet), I was walking with the exhibitor as she looked for possible material. Suddenly she stopped, pointed, and said, "Look at that." "That" was the thick dead branch of a shrub, eight feet tall, with fungus growths like mushrooms attached all the way to the curved tip. "There's my main line," she

said. "Now for a base." In a neighbor's potting shed she found three wooden boxes that, placed one on top of the other at different angles, formed a cubistic base in proper scale for the tall, thick branch. (These were later painted a verdigris color.) The next find was some mushroom-shaped pieces of brain coral that had weathered a dark black-green on a terrace. These were grouped on the boxes as a center of interest. All that remained was to find fill-in material. This turned out to be a branch of weathered wood that supported the main line but curved forward to give a dimensional effect, some tall, green, pointed strelitzia leaves, some dried banana leaves the color of the weathered main and supporting line, and the dead sunflower heads mentioned in the section on Collecting for which the exhibitor sent a hurried SOS to her generous friend. These were a perfect addition because they looked like black mushrooms on curving stems.

When it was completed, it filled all the requirements for a modern arrangement—bold in line; an unusual color scheme; and, although extremely large, restrained in quantity of material. An amusing sidelight was that when the taxi driver, who had helped her transport all her

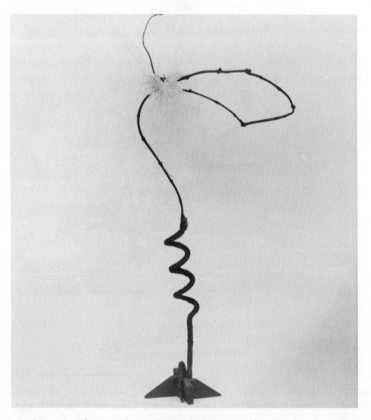

An iron mooring rod is used with blackened wisteria vine to make this abstract arrangement. *Photo by Denby Versfeld Associates. Arrangement by Barbara Corbin.*

material to the exhibition hall, heard that she had won, he said, "What? With all that junk I carried in?"

This particular arrangement was done on a very large scale for a flower show, but modern arrangements for the home use the same format on a scale to fit the background. The driftwood base and cocoanut spathe shown in the color section could be used in a modern house in many ways. It is decorative by itself. With white flowers following the main curve, it could be interpreted as a breaking wave. With daffodils and ivy, it would be a springtime arrangement.

Natural material like driftwood, gnarled roots, cocoanut spathes, rocks, and containers of pottery, glass, or lucite make interesting modern containers. But, also, classic containers like an usabata, an Etruscan cup, or an Egyptian urn that have bold lines are inspiring.

Modern arrangements call for bold foliage such as sansevieria, aspidistra, dracaena, monstera, palmetto, and the bare branches of trees and vines. Flowers with clean-cut lines like anthurium, calla lilies, strelitzia, poker plant, and ginger are also used, along with most fruit.

Abstract Arrangements

All contemporary abstract art is *modern,* but all *modern art* is not abstract. This is because there is not always a dividing line between modern and traditional arrangements. As we said before, a modern arrangement may have the bold line and clean-cut design, yet the elements may be arranged in a traditional way, with the eye radiating from a center of interest.

In an abstract arrangement, however, there is nothing of the traditional. It is a nonrepresentational design in which the elements are arranged to suit the designer. The further from conventional the arrangement is, the more abstract it becomes. Instead of the eye following along traditional lines, in an abstract arrangement the eye can start anywhere in the arrangement and have an easy path from one place to another.

Space is extremely important in an abstract design. Areas of shape, color, and texture must be balanced with voids. Voids are not *in* the arrangement simply because of the placement of flowers but are a part of it. The voids are planned as a definite part of the design.

You can use almost anything in an abstract arrangement that will contribute to the balancing of spaces and solids—even that which is discouraged in other types of arrangement. Such things as wisteria vine, cane, and forsythia wands are often bent to enhance a design and may be painted or bleached. A single flower, minus stem and with no relation to other plant material, is often used as a solid. Old iron in a fanciful shape, graduated blocks of slate or coral, or glass slag can serve as containers.

There are two types of abstract arrangements: A *nonobjective* abstract arrangement simply divides space by line, shape, and color without any particular subject in mind.

A *subjective* abstract arrangement does not represent a visual likeness, but is related to a subject by the artist's inner vision in an impressionistic form.

If making an abstract arrangement seems confusing at first, a further study of abstract painting or sculpture will clarify the patterns. The great joy in making such arrangements is the absolute complete self-expression it allows. Unlike other areas of flower arranging, the opinion of the viewer is immaterial. It is only the satisfaction achieved by experimenting with the relationship of the different parts of the design that matters. Since no one but the arranger knows the effect he has in mind, it is conceded by many that abstract arrangements should not be judged in competition in flower shows.

While abstract arranging is appealing to many, it is unfortunate that in some flower show schools and judges' councils abstract arranging has become so "chic" that arrangers who don't do abstracts are considered old-fashioned. My feeling is that, if it appeals to you, by all means have the joy of doing it but, if it doesn't, remember that just as in the art world we need Wyeths and Picassos, in the flower world we need both traditional and modern artists.

Ikebana

No flower-arranging book today would be complete without some discussion of *Ikebana*—the term used in Japan for the art of flower arranging. But because of the amount of studying needed to fully understand its symbolism and the meticulous placement of the component parts of an arrangement, we cannot go into complete detail here. For the serious student, it is a fascinating lifetime study. For the average arranger, who masters just one of the traditional forms, there will be a sound basis of line, rhythm, balance, and proportion in design to guide him in many varieties of arrangements.

The art of flower arrangement was introduced to Japan in the sixth century by priests and scholars who learned it studying in China. From that time it has been an important influence in the lives of Japanese people. From early childhood they are instructed in *Ikebana*. Calmness, serenity, and spiritual reverence for nature in all its forms are stressed. From palaces and castles to the poorest homes, a flower arrangement has the place of honor in a niche called a Tokonoma. No temple is without symbolic arrangements.

The Japanese make use of all plant material. No flower or plant is too humble to be elevated to a picture of rare beauty. Unlike Western custom, they even use damaged leaves or flowers for a more realistic approach to nature. In addition to flowers they use branches in all forms—bare, flowering, and leaf bearing—and the leaves of plants like iris and aspidistra.

The first flower-arranging school in Japan was the *Ikenobo School*, established thirteen hundred years ago. It is still one of the prominent schools. There are hundreds of schools today, among the better known, the *Sogetsu School* and the *O'Hara School*, which now have branches in the United States. Each school may emphasize different styles, but all styles are based on an asymmetrical triangle with branches of unequal length. There are Japanese names for these branches, but for us it is easier to think of them as "heaven," "man," and "earth."

The longest branch, *heaven,* is one and a half times or more the height or width of the container, depending on the container's size and shape. It curves to the right or left but is placed in the container so that its tip is over its base.

The *man,* or middle branch, is two thirds the height of the heaven branch and is placed against, and slightly to the rear of, the heaven branch.

The lowest, or *earth* branch, is two thirds the length of the man branch and is placed at the base of the other two, curving outward to form the base of the triangle.

An Ikebana arrangement may consist of just these three branches. Or each of the three may be supported by others, making sure that the added branches must not detract from the main ones, and an unequal number are used. Flowers can also be used to support the main line.

R.H.C.

The first style of the Ikenobo School was called RIKKA. The arrangements were very large, the design intricate and classic. They were best suited to temples and palaces. As the love of flower arranging grew among the people, a simpler classic form evolved from RIKKA called SHOKA. This is what we think of today as the basic heaven, man, and earth design.

As Western influence began to be felt in Japan, two new styles developed. NAGEIRE is sometimes known as "throw in" because it looks unstudied. However, each piece of plant material is carefully placed in relation to each other and to the container. The effect is casual, and Nageire arrangements are noted for requiring a small amount of material. Often a carefully chosen graceful branch will be placed upright or to cascade from the mouth of a tall container with a few blossoms at its base.

The other style is MORIBANA. Again, as Western influence was felt in Japanese houses Moribana arrangements were made to be seen from all sides, as opposed to those used in a Tokonoma arrangement which are viewed from the front only. This style is as popular as it is informal and one of the easiest to learn. Like Shoka and Nageire, Moribana is based on the asymmetrical triangle and arranged in a low, flat container. These arrangements are apt to incorporate more flowers in the design than in some of the other styles.

With the coming of World War II, Japanese flower arrangements underwent yet another change. This was the introduction of Abstract and Free Style arrangements. One reason given me on a visit to the Sogetsu School in Tokyo was that, during the war, gardens were not cultivated and forests were depleted. There was a dearth of plant material so that a wide variety of nonplant material—metal, wire, plastic, and metal machinery parts—were used in designs. These could not follow the traditional designs but offered an opportunity to create individual designs of great originality. These designs also fit into the avant-garde approach of the changing modern world.

The type of container also changed for these new arrangements. Instead of the traditional usabatas, incense burners, metal or ceramic boats, and low ceramic containers, those for the new-style arrangements were made of many shapes and materials, often improvised from household containers or using no container at all. Recently I saw an exceptionally beautiful free-style arrangement which used for its container a black tray from a local supermarket combined with a tall container from an exclusive Japanese shop.

After the war, many American wives who accompanied their husbands to Japan with the Army of Occupation became fascinated with Ikebana and studied it while they were there. On their return to the United States, some of the more talented started giving lectures and holding classes in Ikebana. Their enthusiasm infected their audiences and students, and Ikebana International was organized. Today it is worldwide. There are many qualified teachers in the United States today, as well as branches of some of the Japanese schools.

For anyone interested in the study of Ikebana, I would suggest contacting a state garden club for information regarding teachers and schools in the nearest location. It is important to do some research on the teachers and classes suggested because, unfortunately, while some are excellent others are not up to the high standard desired. A teacher of Ikebana should not only be able to impart information, but should also be able to instill the atmosphere of calmness and serenity that is a true part of the Japanese art. Recently I heard a student say, "When I go to my teacher's house for a lesson, I feel all tension begin to fade as I enter the door, and all the time I am there I feel as though I hadn't a care in the world." Fortunate is the pupil who has such a teacher.

There is something in Ikebana to appeal to any flower arranger, whether it is the peaceful style of the classic arrangements, the gayer Moribana or Nagiere, or the challenging abstract and free-style designs. No flower arranger should miss the reward of exposure to it.

3
Arrangements for the Home

Arrangements for the Outside Entrance and Hall

The Outside Entrance

There is no place in a house that is not appropriate for flower arrangements, including bathrooms, kitchens, and entrance doorways. An arrangement of plants and flowers outside the entrance to your house is a wonderful way to give a gracious welcome to visitors. The arrangement should be in keeping with the period of the house.

For instance, for an *Early American* house you could use an iron grate (the kind made for burning coal in a fireplace) on the doorstep. You can change the material with the seasons—flowering branches in the spring, geraniums in the summer, autumn leaves in the fall, and evergreens in the winter.

For a *Victorian* house, a pair of round metal urns, which graced a garden around the turn of the century, placed on either side of the door could be planted with ivy geraniums, begonias, or fuchsia. In the winter you could substitute a pair of small evergreen trees.

For an *eighteenth-century* house, you might make a pair of tapered ivy trees. These look impressive but are quite simple to make. To do so, select matching pots (they may be of metal, pottery, or clay, either plain or painted). Make a cone of chicken wire the diameter and height that you want, and fill it with moistened sphagnum moss. Sink the cones into the soil in the pots, and plant ivy around them. Also plant rooted ivy cuttings in the sphagnum moss. As the ivy in the pot grows, train it around the cone and soon, with the cuttings, the wire will be covered, and you will have a most decorative pair of trees. When you water them, be sure to moisten the moss inside the cone also.

A ceramic lavabo or terra-cotta wall pockets would be attractive attached to the stucco walls of the *Spanish-type* houses of the Southwest. Soft green succulents spilling from these against the white or subtly-colored walls would make a fascinating combination of color or texture.

In the South I saw a stunning six-foot-tall arrangement of tropical greens against the white stucco house wall. The container was a round black-iron hibachi placed on a rough coral brick, and consisted of five-foot-tall sansevieria, sago palm, palmetto, pittosporum, with a banana blossom at the focal point.

Containers

Some containers that are appropriate for outside entrances are jardinieres (I remember one such filled with eight-foot sprays of rambler roses on the doorstep of a house in which there was to be a wedding), old churns, coal scuttles, or large glass bottles. And don't forget baskets which come in so many shapes and colors that your choice is practically unlimited.

The Entrance Hall

Not many of us in these busy days have time to completely fill all the rooms of our houses with flowers every day, but the entrance hall, or foyer, is one area that is important. It is often the only room that a stranger sees. It is the room that first welcomes a visitor, or welcomes the family home from daily trips to office, school, business, or market. The welcome should be a cheery one, and nothing can give this feeling more than flowers and plants. Even in the tiniest hall there is a place for living plant material.

One entrance hall that I never enter without being impressed is tiny and elliptically shaped with stairs curving across the back. The only thing furnishing the hall, and the first thing that you see as the door is opened, is a wide shelf on brackets against the stairwell. On the shelf, in an interesting tall brass bottle with a narrow neck, is an arrangement of plants growing in water.

Growing plants in water is a very satisfactory way to make an arrangement because the cut pieces of plant material root in the water, and the arrangement will last indefinitely. As opposed to when you have cut flowers in water, for an arrangement of growing plants the container should not be transparent, because the roots are not attractive to look at and the water is apt to become discolored. A jar set inside an attractive container is a good way to hide the roots. Put a piece of charcoal in the water to keep it sweet. The water needs to be replaced only as it evaporates. A pinholder is helpful for holding the stems in a widemouthed container.

The arrangement in this hall was of sansevieria and pothos. The tall swordlike sansevieria leaves made a contrast to the heart-shaped ones of the pothos trailing down the side of the bottle. On either side of the brass bottle of greens was a handsome brass snail. The effect was dramatic and very simple.

Other plants that root well and can be arranged like flowers while still growing in water are aceuba, philodendron, ivy, tradescantia, Chinese evergreen, and coleus.

Arrangements of plants growing in water are very practical in a hall because they last a long time. You can arrange a variety of plants as you would cut flowers.

A narrow rectangular container of the shape usually known as a "planter" would be a good size and shape for a narrow hall table. Chinese evergreen for height, graceful sprays of ivy at the sides, and begonia leaves and coleus for a center of interest would be an arrangement that could be fastened in a pinholder. If you pick ivy from outdoors, cut it before the weather is too cold, and cut mature growth rather than new green tendrils.

In a hall that is large enough, there is nothing more cheerful than a bright, splashy bouquet. Often a hall table is placed under a mirror and this is a challenging place for flowers—challenging because the arrangement will be reflected in the mirror, and the back must be as attractive as the front. You can accomplish this by making the arrangement as though it was to be seen only from the front. Then, when it is in place, take extra leaves and flowers and fill in the back, looking in the mirror as you do it to make sure that the reflected flower picture has good design.

Since a pineapple is the symbol of hospitality, a fruit arrangement featuring a pineapple would be a good choice. For more details on arranging fruit, see page 68.

Using
a Niche

If, as in many halls, you are fortunate to have a small niche built into the wall, you have a little stage, and you can let your imagination have full rein setting little scenes. Maybe it's a terrifically cold winter and you'd love to take off for the tropics, but you can't. Bring the tropics to you for a while by bringing out shells, starfish, sea fans, pieces of colored sea glass, and any other related objects you have collected. Line the niche with paper to suggest sea color, cover the floor of the niche with sand, and find some green material that looks as if it might be underwater growth. (Small, crinkly spinach leaves are one example.) Put this in a pinholder and hide the holder with stones and shells. Experiment with placing your other objects until you have created a tropical underwater scene. Then when the sleet is pelting against the windows and you feel blue, you can stand in front of the niche and get a glimpse of the tropics and feel cheerful again.

Perhaps you have one of the many lovely figures of St. Francis with his birds. You can line the floor of the niche with moss, and make a shady glen for St. Francis to stand in, with pieces of foliage to simulate trees, and a few little flowers nestled at his feet. You can buy tiny pinholders less than half an inch in diameter and fasten them in bottle tops for miniature cup pinholders. Hide them under the moss.

If you don't want to go to the trouble of arranging scenes in your niche, you could do what I do. In mine I usually keep two sentimental objects—a gray-blue Copenhagen narrow-necked vase that one of my daughters brought to me from her first trip abroad, and, in the same colors, a little ceramic fledgling bird with upraised beak that my ten-year-old grandson gave me last Christmas, saying, "I hope you like it. It cost a whole dollar." In the vase I put an especially pretty hybrid rose from the garden, a late spray from the climbers, or a few sprigs of unusual foliage that have caught my eye—in fact, anything I want to enjoy by itself. The little bird, placed so that he is looking up at them, seems to enjoy them too.

Living Room Arrangements

A living room decorated in perfect taste can be as cold and impersonal as a department store display without the addition of some living plant material. On the other hand, a cottage room furnished with nondescript hand-me-downs, but filled with flowers and plants, gives a lasting impression of warmth and coziness.

Admittedly it takes time to arrange flowers, and most of us are busy. For this reason I think it is a very good idea to sit down and decide where in your living room flowers look best. Then deliberately decide on containers that fit these places and plan the mechanics necessary for them. Then on a busy day you can whip up arrangements in no time. This does not mean denying yourself the pleasure of dreaming up something new and different when you have some leisure. It is simply a suggestion to save time on a busy day so that there will be flowers in your room when otherwise you might not have any.

I have two containers that are my standbys. One is the bronze lamp vase that I have already described in the section on Containers. This stands on a pedestal table against a celadon-green wall. The other is a hexagonal fluted pewter sugar bowl, and is on an end table. These are my "busy day" containers (although on other days I may have fun planning something more elaborate in them).

In the summer, which is my busiest time, I make an arrangement in the lamp-base container of greens, such as euonymus or laurel, which last a long time and provide perfect backgrounds for flowers. I happen to have a hedge of hybrid day lilies, which I think are one of the most satisfactory flowers to grow as they have a succession of bloom from June to September and come in shades of yellow, apricot, orange, mahogany, coral, crimson, and scarlet. Each morning I gather these flower heads (they last a day out of water) and wire each to a florists' pick. Then I stick them into the green background, according to my mood of the day—sometimes in a mass, sometimes in a curve. Sometimes in shades of yellow to brown, sometimes in shades of pink to red, and sometimes a combination of many colors. It takes only a few minutes each morning to discard the dead heads and rewire fresh ones onto the pick.

In the sugar bowl I usually put garden flowers of one kind—petunias, rambler roses, daisies, and the like.

In Bermuda, where we live most winters, my "busy day" arrangement is of pittosporum, and instead of the day lilies I use hibiscus blossoms which also last a day out of water.

Using Furniture and Fixtures

Living room *mantels* are interesting places to put flowers. The important thing is to make sure that any flower arrangement balances other accessories in the overall design. You can do this by making a low rectangular arrangement and placing it underneath a rectangular painting. Or, if there is an oval mirror or framed portrait hanging in the center, a crescent-shaped arrangement underneath, following the lines of the mirror or frame would be suitable. An arrangement on one end of a mantelpiece can be balanced by a grouping of candlesticks on the other end. Or, if you have two identical containers, you can make arrangements in each of them for each end of the mantel. These arrangements should be identical in shape and size, but not necessarily identical material, although related in color.

There are many twin containers suitable for mantels. For Early American and Colonial houses there are pewter mugs, cheese boxes, luster pitchers and bowls, and candle molds. For eighteenth-century houses there are Chinese porcelain bowls, porcelain urns, delicate bronze containers, and, for Victorian houses, fan-shaped vases, metal urns with marble bases, alabaster compotes, and figurines holding a small bowl aloft.

A living room *coffee table* is a popular place for flower arrangements. The important thing to remember when doing one is to keep the arrangement in proportion to the size of the table. If it is a small table, you could make a miniature arrangement; but some coffee tables are quite large, in which case the arrangement should be large too. The arrangement should also be in proper scale with the other accessories on the table, and the material should be in good scale with the container.

For a coffee table in an Early American house, a pewter inkwell with miniature geraniums or a pewter porringer with pansies would look nice. You might use a pressed-glass spoonholder with a bouquet of small garden flowers. For an eighteenth-century house a small bowl of Export china filled with miniature roses would be lovely, and in a Victorian house a vase shaped like a small hand filled with a cornucopia (typical of that period) holding a little bunch of lilies of the valley, violets, and fuchsia would be fragrant as well as pretty. In a modern house, try an ebony box, sitting on a white wrought-iron coffee table. Its upraised lid could form a background for a few white cyclamen blossoms or other interesting white flowers.

Instead of a screen or pleated fan in front of a *fireplace* opening, try using a brass kettle filled with autumn leaves, or a huge white fluted clamshell filled with greens. At Halloween it would be amusing to put a lighted pumpkin jack-o'-lantern in the opening.

Contemporary Homes Need Special Attention

In the living rooms of modern houses, it is particularly important to consider the dimensional qualities in arrangements since they are often placed against glass walls or on room dividers where they are seen from both sides. Because there is a transition from indoors to outdoors in these houses, natural containers like stumps, driftwood, and roots are very suitable. This doesn't mean the container has to be rough in texture, although it could be. Wood can be peeled, waxed, and polished so that it is compatible with the finest furniture. Containers of metal or pottery and Oriental containers of metal or bamboo also look good in contemporary surroundings.

The importance of flowers in a living room was graphically illustrated to me recently when I was one of the hostesses in a home on an Open House Tour. In the drawing room on either side of the fireplace were lighted shelves holding priceless antiquities dating from 1200 and 1300 B.C. My duty was to explain (and guard) these objects.

In front of the fireplace was a low table with a massive silver bowl containing a mass of gorgeous yellow hybrid freesias. This caused so much interest and favorable comment that I found myself spending more time explaining what "those beautiful flowers" were than I did explaining the history of the antiquities.

Dining Room Arrangements and Table Settings

One of the most creative and challenging tasks is to set a table. And never has it been easier to set lovely tables than at the present time with the wealth of new "no iron" cloths and attractive table mats that have come on the market in the past few years. It takes only a little imagination and ingenuity to have different effects that will please your family and guests.

Instead of dreading the routine chore and having the family sitting down to the same table appointments each meal, why not make it fun? Say to yourself, "We're having fish tonight. I think I'll put that fishnet in the garage over the green plastic cloth, and bring in the Japanese glass fishing balls from the porch to use in the center of the table." Really not much more work, is it? Or, "We're having spaghetti tonight. I'll use the straw table mats, straw-covered wine bottles for candlesticks, and a wicker tray of grapes that will double as a centerpiece and dessert."

Planning the Table Setting

There are many things that govern a table setting. How many people are to be served? Is it seated or buffet? Where is the table—kitchen, dining room, porch, or terrace? Is it for breakfast, lunch, or dinner? Is it a party or a family meal?

The size of the table and how many are to be served are the first things to be considered. If a table seats six, and four to six people will be served, the meal would probably be seated. If there are more people expected, the dinner will probably be buffet.

For a seated meal the table accessories—china, glass, and silver—are placed the same, whether the meal is breakfast, lunch, or dinner. The centerpiece can be in the middle, with each place setting equidistant around it, or it can be at one end, with the place settings along each side. If it is in the middle, it must be low enough so that people can see over it. (This can be accomplished by extending an arrangement at the sides and keeping it low in the middle.)

Plates are placed equidistant from each other, with forks at the left and knives and spoons at the right. The waterglass goes on the right (with wineglasses, if used, slightly to the right and a little in front of the waterglass), above the tip of the knife. Butter plates and napkins are at the left. Whether the corner of the napkin points toward the plate or away from it is a matter of personal preference.

For a buffet table, the centerpiece is usually placed at the back if the table is against a wall; or in the middle if it is in the center of the room. There is really no set rule. Its placement is governed by the placement of the other serving pieces on the table. But remember: Everything must be balanced.

Tablecloths— Choosing the Right Color

The cloth is the background for a table setting. I use the word "cloth" loosely, because you can also use the bare polished table top, a glass top, or mats. Soft colors are easiest to work with, although it is exciting to accept the challenge of a brilliant color. Do have as many colored cloths as you can. As we said before, not only are there many inexpensive and easy-to-care-for cloths now available, but you can explore remnant counters for material to make them. You may not have a great variety of china or patterns of glass, but with different color combinations in table linens and flowers, it is easy to change the whole effect of your table.

If you want to be really elegant, and don't mind a little extra laundering, damask cloths, left from your trousseau (or your mother's) or picked up for a song at auction sales, dye beautifully. When cut they also make lovely circular cloths.

Many people have gold-and-white china. It is nice on a white cloth, but how much lovelier it would be on a soft green cloth with a centerpiece of yellow acacia and daffodils; or try a dull gold cloth with an arrangement of daisies and yellow privet.

If blue is your favorite color, plan to use your blue cloths for breakfast or lunch, as this color fades in artificial light. If your china is decorated with blue, use warm colors with it at night. There is a Wedgwood pattern of white plates circled with an embossed design of blue grapes. For lunch they would be lovely on pale blue mats with a centerpiece of forget-me-nots, violets, and heather. At night this combination would look dull. Instead, a pink cloth with heather, pink sweet peas, deep-rose roses, and purple anemones would be lovely.

Tableware
and Setting

You don't have to have expensive china and glassware to have beautiful tables. The shops are full of merchandise with moderate prices and good design. The latter is most important. The less decoration the china has, the more ways you can use it.

There are several questions that always arise in discussions of table settings which I'd like to discuss.

"Can you use place mats for dinner?" No rule says you can't. Solid backgrounds such as a tablecloth or the natural wood are usually used at dinner because they are less distracting and more restful; a good choice at night when people may be tired. However, if you want to use mats, go ahead.

Another question is, "Can you use candles at lunch?" The general rule is not to use candles before dusk. After all, why have them? You don't need them for light, and if you want them for color, there are other ways to introduce it.

In every discussion of table settings, the question arises, "What is the difference between formal and informal?" This is not an easy question to answer because there are no rigid rules. Rather it is a quality that you feel. Informal settings are gay. They may have a feeling of amusement. There is a relaxed feeling in an informal table. Figurines used as a centerpiece may set a mood or tell a story. Formal tables on the other hand have a feeling of elegant simplicity. Without being ornate, they look "dressed up." Flower arrangements are usually in more conventional containers. Napkins are larger. Where possible, crystal and fine china are used. Added pieces such as service plates and finger bowls may be used.

The Importance
of Height

A general rule for table arrangements is that the arrangements should be low enough so as not to obstruct the view of people seated opposite each other. It is disconcerting to have to peek around a bowl of flowers to talk to someone on the other side of you. People ask, "If you are using a large container like a soup tureen, or a large bowl, don't the flowers have to be tall to be in good proportion to the container?" The answer to this is, keep the flowers short in height in the middle, but extend them at the sides so that you have horizontal proportion instead of vertical. A glass bowl of gladioli with spiky flowers like snapdragons, heather, stock, delphinium, and annual larkspur are good for making this type of arrangement. If you don't have spiky flowers, you can get the same proportional effect with foliage.

One of the most exciting and challenging table centerpieces I ever did was governed by the height of the table arrangement. For a recent visit of Queen Elizabeth and Prince Philip to Bermuda, members of the Garden Club of Bermuda were invited to do the flowers at Government House. My assignment was to do the table flowers for the dinner for the Queen. The table was very long and quite narrow, and the chairs were carved and high-backed and upholstered in an almost magenta color. In the center, in front of the place where the Queen was to be seated, was a very tall silver candelabrum, ornately carved up the pedestal with what looked like curved silver claws (the candles were well above the heads of anyone seated). The strict rule given me was that the flowers should not interfere with anyone's view of the Queen.

I was fortunate in my material in that I found two key things: snapdragons almost the exact shade of the magenta chairs, and pots of staghorn fern which a neighbor allowed me to cut. The formation of the ends of the fern was almost the same shape as the silver "claws" on the candelabrum.

I didn't use containers, but concealed blocks of Oasis with flowers and fern. The arrangement started on either side of the candelabrum, with the snapdragons and fern decreasing in height and color (ending in pale pink). The butler was setting the table as I worked, and every once in a while I would say, "Am I keeping this low enough?" and he would gravely sit down in one of the chairs and say, "Yes, Madam. It is quite satisfactory." I must admit that when I was finished, I sat in the Queen's chair and touched each of the wineglasses!

This is the easiest way to make an arrangement for the center of the dining table.

1. Put whatever you are using for mechanics—Oasis or pinholder—in the container.
2. Then put a spiky-form flower approximately 12″ high in the center for the top line.

3. Next put a longer spiky form extending out each side.

You now have formed the outline of a triangular design, with a horizontal hypotenuse. Complete the side of the arrangement facing you. This is less confusing than if you keep turning the container around and around as you work.

4. Support the original spiky flowers with buds and other spiky forms. Establish a center of interest in the middle.

5. Now turn the container around and do the other side in the same manner. The two sides do not have to be identical. In fact it is more interesting *not* to have them identical, although the same color scheme should prevail. In an arrangement in shades of pink,

rose, and lavender, you could have pink roses at the focal point on one side and purple pansies at the focal point of the other.

6. For a finishing touch, turn each end of the arrangement toward you and fill in where necessary.

An exception to the rule of keeping low flowers in the center of the table is the use of a tall flowering branch or a piece of driftwood with flowers at the base. The view is not then obstructed since you can see through the branches.

Breakfast Tables
and
Breakfast Trays

With the busy lives that most of us lead, a leisurely breakfast seems to be impractical. That is why it is nice to make an occasion of the times when the family can be together at the breakfast table on a weekend, a holiday morning, or when there are guests. Because it may be infrequent, a leisurely breakfast at a gaily set table seems like a special treat.

A breakfast table should be cheerful and have a "wake up" feeling. China, glasses, and linen should be sparkling clean and colors bright. This is a time for informal and gay table settings. You might, for instance, use yellow Quimper pottery plates, with their touches of dark green, dark blue, and orange, on a green cloth. For a centerpiece you might use two painted peasant figures, to relate to the ones on the plates, standing by a low arrangement of lemons, limes, kumquats, and blue grapes.

Or, you could start with a figurine suggesting early morning sounds, like ceramic roosters, birds, or ducks, and build the table setting around them. Try putting white ceramic roosters on either side of a circle of white egg cups holding red begonia, and use white pottery plates on a red cloth. Or, you might choose straw place mats, green and white plates, and a straw basket of daisies for a centerpiece.

In more formal houses, china like the well-known "moss rose" pattern, would be pretty on pink linen place mats, with a bowl of just-picked garden roses for a centerpiece.

Even on busy mornings, when breakfast may be a hurried one at the kitchen counter bar, a copper coffeepot full of marigolds at the end, repeating the color of orange-juice-filled glasses, would make the morning seem more cheerful; a freshly picked bunch of mint in a tall sugar shaker would add its fragrance to that of the brewing coffee.

Sometimes it is fun to pamper someone by serving breakfast in bed on a tray. If you do, plan the appointments as carefully as though you were setting a table, and be sure to add a little arrangement. This should be something that won't tip over easily; try pansies in a small brown luster pitcher, Johnny-jump-ups in a little pewter sugar bowl, or some mixed small flowers in a child's silver mug. Invalids need trays for most meals and it would give them great pleasure if there was a different little nosegay on each. It is nice to make these fragrant. A few lilies of the valley in a silver pepper shaker, some garden pinks in a pressed-glass toothpick holder, or a few sprigs of mock orange in a gold-and-white demitasse cup can do wonders to perk up drooping spirits.

Dining in the Kitchen

In many houses built within recent years, a dining room as such has been eliminated, and a dining area is incorporated as part of a family kitchen or as an alcove in the living room. If the kitchen dining room is furnished with sturdy comfortable furniture, and the walls are wood paneled or painted, table settings would be gay and informal. However, in some houses the dining area of a kitchen has glass walls, a floor garden of plants, and quite formal wrought-iron furniture. In this case, more elegant table settings would be appropriate.

If the kitchen dining area has a fireplace, you can make a container to relate to the color of the bricks. To do this, turn a conventional flowerpot upside down, and fasten its matching saucer on the top with Stickum or glue. This makes a sturdy compote, ready to be filled with colorful fruit and/or vegetables or bright garden flowers.

Containers related to the kitchen are fun to use for kitchen dining tables—a bread tray, a copper pot, a wooden dough board, or an iron kettle are good possibilities. Here, too, is the place for discovering that fascinating vegetable forms—spinach, beet, broccoli and rhubarb leaves, artichokes, gourds, brussels sprouts, and cabbage—are all lovely in arrangements.

For a dining table in a living room, since there is usually not as much space for a large table, using a candelabrum for both candles and flowers, as described later in this chapter, is ideal. Good too, for a table like this, is an arrangement either of early spring green or flowering branches with an accent of flowers, as it gives a feeling of space.

In a dining area that is part of a living room, the furnishings of the room would be the key to the table setting.

**Lunch
and
Dinner
Tables**

Although in many ways table settings for lunch and dinner are similar, there are some definite differences. One is *color*. Because natural light is strongest at noon, lunch is a time when you can use colors that

A gay arrangement using the primary colors of red carnations, red-spotted rubrum lilies, yellow daffodils, and blue irises. Notice that the use of two bases gives stability and distinction. *Photo by Roche. Arrangement by Myra Brooks.*

would lose their intensity under artificial light, such as all tones of blue, violet, mauve, orchid, burgundy, hyacinth, and olive green.

Another difference between lunch and dinner settings is *scale*. Lunch plates are smaller than dinner plates, and lunch napkins are smaller than dinner ones. While tumblers can be used at lunch, usually taller goblets are used at dinner. Although it is fine to use table mats for dinner, they are more often used at lunch. Since candles are not needed for actual lighting at lunch time, they are not required. Candles are used at dinner because they provide a most flattering light.

**Patio
Tables**

When you set a table on a terrace or patio, it is necessary to consider the wind. Table appointments should not be fragile. The centerpiece must be such that it won't blow away. If candles are used, they must be protected so that they won't blow out or drip on the table. There are several ways to use candles successfully. One is to use them in tall hurricane shades. Drill holes in a board to hold candles, and surround it at the sides and back with a tall, curved piece of transparent plastic to shield the candles from the prevailing wind. I recently discovered something I have found invaluable. At a restaurant-supply store I bought a number of small juice glasses and a supply of food-warming candles. The candles, placed in the glasses (the flame being below the edge of the glass), burn for ten hours. You can cluster these in attractive designs on either an indoor or outdoor table. They also solve the problem on tables at a banquet or dinner dance, as placed at intervals on a long table they give light for the whole evening, whereas regular candles sometimes burn out before the festivities of the evening are over.

**Outdoor
Table Settings**

It is fun to do tables out of doors, as the surrounding landscape is your background, and you are not limited as to color, texture, or period. One outdoor table I did started with an unusual coral fan that I found in Bermuda. I was intrigued with its dimensional quality and the way part of it curved like a sail in the wind. This gave me the idea of making a "boat" centerpiece by using it with the cocoanut spathe. The spathe wouldn't rest squarely on the table, so I found a piece of drift-wood that was flat and fastened the spathe to it with Stickum. I also used Stickum to fasten the fan to the boat. An arching spray of minia-ture pink cymbidium orchids from a neighbor made the "passengers." I had a pink cloth and some smoky purple glasses that related to the colors in the fan. When I found the shell-shaped crinkly glass plates in the same purple and pink colors in a gift shop, I remembered some oyster shells we had picked up on a fishing dock in Baltimore thinking they would be nice containers for seafood cocktails. I got them out, scrubbed them, and my table was set.

Buffet Tables

A buffet-type setting may be used for any meal. It is an intriguing problem in design; for, in addition to a flower arrangement, you also have to place silver, china, napkins, serving dishes, and, if it is in the evening, candles. The design must have good balance, and the different parts must relate in color, form, and texture.

Because there are so many different objects to place in relation to each other, it is more difficult to set a buffet table artistically than one at which people are seated, and where place settings are symmetrical. Also, while food for a seated dinner may be served by a waitress or from a serving table, the food is part of the design on a buffet table. At a flower show, in a class for buffet tables, the judges consider all these things, and many times, in a close decision, the ribbon goes to the one that has the greatest number of objects placed in the best design.

The color scheme for another buffet table I did was suggested by the floral design on the white china, in which there was blue, lavender, yel-low, and coral. Because the hostess wanted to use a pewter candela-brum, she chose pewter serving pieces and used dull stainless-steel flat-ware instead of silver. She chose a lavender cloth because it emphasized the more subtle coloring in the china, and was a good con-trast with the soft gray of the pewter. For a container, she used a hex-agonal pewter sugar bowl and emphasized bright colors in the arrange-ment to counteract the "nonevening" color of the lavender cloth. The yellow freesia and acacia and coral azalea were definitely needed. The pewter flower container was related in design to the salt and pepper shakers, which in turn related to the design of the candelabrum. The candelabrum was placed off center, an important maneuver to balance the visual weight of the flowers.

**Creating Space
with a Candelabrum**

Sometimes there are so many objects to go on a buffet table that there is little room for the flower arrangement. One way to solve this is to use a candelabrum instead of candlesticks. You can buy small glass bowls with a little projection at the bottom that fits into a candlestick. Remove the center candle of the candelabrum, put the bowl in its place, fill it with Oasis, and make a flower arrangement of proper size in the bowl, between the candles. For a lunch buffet where you are not using candles, you can still use the candelabrum, putting the little bowls in each candle opening. This makes a very pretty and unusual arrangement that takes up little room on the table.

If you can't find the glass bowls, there are metal holders, with the same projection to fit in a candlestick, that are sold at florist shops. They are a little more difficult to use, however, as you have to conceal the metal holder with flowers and foliage. If you can't find either of these containers, you can use a piece of Oasis. Soak a two- or three-inch cube of Oasis and wrap it in foil or plastic, tying it firmly like a package with heavy thread. (The wrapping is to make sure no water will drip on the tablecloth.) Take two wires about fifteen inches long, and insert them at right angles through the center of the Oasis. Place the package of Oasis on top of the empty candle opening and fasten it there by binding the ends of the wire round and round the top of the supporting candlestick.

In the Oasis you can have an attractive arrangement with a mere handful of flowers. Establish a design by placing a short spiky flower at the top and sides. (If you have trouble inserting the stems through the covering, make a little hole with a nail or other sharp object.) Spiky flowers that are good are the tips or sidepieces of delphiniums or annual larkspur, side shoots of heather, or buds of spray chrysanthemums. Don't be afraid to cut the stems short, as you have to keep the arrangement in scale so that it looks like part of the candelabrum unit. You can use the larger flowers of spray chrysanthemums or clusters of florets from the base of stalks of stock, delphinium, and snapdragon to fill the center. Flowers with round forms and stems sturdy enough to stick in the Oasis are sweet peas, tiny roses, daisies, and stephanotis.

Fruits can also be used with a candelabrum. Think of the candelabrum and fruit as one arrangement, with the candles as the high point. Place the candelabrum on a base, a polished board, a mirror, or a silver tray turned upside down. Arrange fruit selected for the desired color scheme on the base at each side of the candelabrum. The scale of fruit should be small—seckel pears, lady apples, clusters of cherries, small limes, and small green grapes are all suitable. Make the transition from the fruit at the base to the candles using sprays of berried vines winding up to them. Cotoneaster with coral berries, fire thorn with orange, viburnum with purplish-black, bayberry with gray, poke-weed with purplish-black, juniper with silvery-gray, bittersweet with red and orange, and rose-colored rose hips are just some of the berries in color ranges available. Vines to use with them would be clematis, miniature ivy, tradescantia, and grape ivy. The vines can be in cup pinholders concealed by the fruit.

Impromptu and Winter Arrangements

Someone who lives in New England once said to me, "What can you do for a table arrangement between Christmas and early spring when there are no garden flowers, and others are so expensive?"

There are a number of solutions. This is the time to look around the house and find something you are using as decoration somewhere other than the dining room. Perhaps with the addition of just a little live material it will make a pleasing centerpiece.

You may have an antique compote. Fill it with some of the luscious-looking artificial lemons and green grapes that are available, add a few real limes (artificial ones never seem to have the natural rich coloring) and, using water picks, add some laurel from the dooryard or sprigs from a house plant. With a pair of Sheffield grape shears thrust in the top, it would be an inviting centerpiece that would last a long time.

In the library there may be a wooden duck decoy. Bring him to the table and let him nestle under an arrangement of dried field material. If you have a copper tray, use some leaves like aspidistra or bird's-nest fern for height, and for flower forms at the base use ruffled round geranium leaves that are tinged with bronze. Some chunks of brown glass added to this would give a distinctive accent.

If you have house plants, you can make a very colorful bouquet in one of the Oasis holders described in the section on Mechanical Aids. Make the horizontal line with ivy, tradescantia, grape ivy, or laurel, and for color in the center use snips of begonia, kalenchoe, African violet, azalea, fuchsia, or cineraria from your plants.

A succession of paper-white narcissus bulbs planted at intervals in low flat containers and brought out at the height of their bloom will give you flowers over a long period. For a more colorful centerpiece, you can buy croton foliage which comes in different colors and lasts a long time. Use them alone with other table appointments to emphasize the color, or combine them with greens or accessories like colored glass, figurines, or a piece of sculpture. And last but not least, there are always forced branches.

An allied problem in table setting is that of the *impromptu* or last-minute arrangement. Probably all of us have had the experience of having unexpected guests for lunch or dinner when there isn't a trace of an arrangement on the dining table.

Just as you have cans of food on a shelf for such an emergency meal, you can be prepared for quick and impromptu table arrangements. Some day when your hands are occupied but your mind is free, dream up some good ideas. Mentally catalog what greens are always available outside. Make a list, mental or otherwise, of containers and mechanics that you can fix quickly and of accessories that are interesting. For instance, you might twist philodendron or ivy around the graceful figurine of a Chinese goddess from your living-room mantel. Or dash out and gather mixed greens for a bouquet in a white soup tureen. Decide on a shallow container that you could use if you have two or three daffodils or roses in bloom. Cut them in different lengths and put them with their foliage in the shallow container placed at one side so that the water forms part of the design. Use a pot of blooming African violets, pot and all placed in a deep bowl.

And don't forget the refrigerator! Grapes, tomatoes, an artichoke or two, spinach leaves, and other edible material, with the addition of greens, would make a lovely centerpiece.

Kitchen
Arrangements

It is more than just a coincidence that in almost every picture you see of a model kitchen in a magazine there is an arrangement of flowers, fruit or vegetables, or a thriving plant. The competent decorators who plan the layouts know that this plant material adds to the charm of the room.

In my kitchen, the feature that gives me the most pleasure is the result of a lucky accident. There is a corner sink, and an angle is formed by two picture windows which look out on a field full of bayberry, juniper, native shrubs, willow trees, and the water of Barnegat Bay. Since this makes a natural landscape background, I felt the triangle formed by the right-angled windows would be an ideal place for flowering plants. My husband was putting a Fiberglas bottom on his boat, and I asked him to make me a Fiberglas tray to fit the angle and to hold plants.

Sad to say, it was not a success for plants because the angles were so sharp that the pots only fit in the center, leaving gaping spaces at the corners. I tried various-sized pots with no success, and finally in disgust I threw the tray in the trash barrel. My husband found it there and, naturally, resenting such treatment of his handiwork rescued it and brought it back. I was a bit remorseful and accepted the challenge of using it. Since then it has been my pride and joy and a conversation piece for everyone who sees it.

For instance, in November and December I keep it full of paperwhite narcissus. To hold the bulbs I use pieces of stone that I have collected from many places. As I stand at the sink and look at the stones, I am transported in memory to the pilgrimage city of Baalbek high on a Lebanon plain; or to the island of Delos in Greece, its sur-

face covered with an Oriental carpet of brightly colored wildflowers and to the inscrutable Sphinx and the pyramids, golden against a vivid blue sky.

Since the Fiberglas tray holds water, I scrub it out and use it as a huge flower container. When the first daffodils come, I make naturalistic clumps with their foliage and buds in pinholders scattered in the tray. Later on in the spring I put flowering branches in pinholders at the edges of the tray, as though they were arching over a pool, and nestle crocuses, grape hyacinths, or violets at their feet. In summer I fill the tray with blocks of Oasis and have a miniature flower garden. Perhaps you could fasten a wide glass shelf to a kitchen window and, using a low flat container, bring winter, spring, and summer bloom to your kitchen, too.

Why not fasten an old-fashioned salt box or coffee grinder to your kitchen wall, and put a water-holding container in it to hold a bouquet of fresh herbs? Or put marigolds, fresh from the garden, into a black iron cooking pot. A bouquet of fragrant fresh mint in a glass pitcher makes a cool-looking spot on a hot day.

Instead of putting cabbage, spinach, tomatoes, and green peppers in the refrigerator as soon as you come from the market, why not take two minutes (and I mean literally that) to curl back the outer leaves of the cabbage so that it looks like a huge green rose, and put it on a breadboard with some of the tomatoes and green peppers piled against it? Clusters of the dark green spinach leaves will give grace to the arrangement. You can enjoy the rich color and form of the vegetables all day until it is time to prepare them for dinner.

If you have two baskets of strawberries, their green hulls still intact, put one on each plate of a scale, tipping the baskets so that some of the berries fall out onto it. They will contribute to the attractiveness of your kitchen, and the berries will taste all the better for dessert that night after being at room temperature all day.

Bedroom Arrangements

The other day I went into a bedroom to leave my coat and was intrigued by an arrangement on a small table. The room was very feminine, and the furniture delicate. On the slender round-topped table were sprays of Sprengeri fern (the kind you usually see garlanding a wedding cake) arranged in a most unusual container. I went closer to examine it and found that it was made by fastening two opaque white goblets base to base (probably with Stickum). It was just right for the room and so unusual that, simple as it was, it immediately caught my attention.

Flower arrangements for a bedroom need not be elaborate. In one's own bedroom they can sometimes be on the sentimental side—for instance, on a dressing table, some lilies of the valley in a silver baby's shoe that was given to your mother when you were born, or, on a bedside table, a mixed bouquet from the garden in the small Victorian vase your grandmother cherished.

Containers that have an association with a bedroom seem a natural choice, like a large perfume bottle with a narrow neck and globular bottom. Ferns planted in antique containers make dainty and long-lasting arrangements for the top of a chest of drawers.

There is a shade of dusty rose that is often found in bedroom chintzes. In the fall, a perfect plant to use for a bedroom that has this color is abelia. This is a shrub with small evergreen leaves that in the summer has small white flowers. In autumn, the flowers fall off, leaving a cluster of dusty rose bracts that look like small flowers.

Once when I was visiting in the South, every morning on my dressing table a triangular mound of fresh hibiscus flower heads was placed under the mirror. This type of simple arrangement would be attractive in a modern house. You could have the same effect in the North using mallow blossoms or the flower heads of day lilies.

A child will be fascinated to have in his bedroom a dish garden of small succulents, particularly when he learns that the plants have such names as peppermint stick, tiger jaws, necklace vine, fairy washboard, tiny Tim, ponytail, or baseball plant. These are all listed in catalogs. He can add sand and flat stones to have the dish garden resemble a Western landscape, and to make it even more realistic he can add tiny cowboy and Indian figures.

It is a nice idea to think of *fragrance* for a bedroom when you are planning outside planting. No one who has slept in a first-floor bedroom, with a bed of rose geranium or nicotiana under the window, will forget the lovely scent on the night air. Nicotiana (tobacco plant) has flowers that open at night and give an exquisite jasminelike fragrance.

White geraniums are related in color and texture to an antique cologne bottle. *Photo by Roche. Arrangement by Katherine N. Cutler.*

Bathroom Arrangements

Flowers in a bathroom? Visitors to Japan, the cradle of the art of flower arrangement, are delighted to find flowers and plants not only in most bathrooms but in the public rest rooms as well.

You naturally think of water in connection with a bathroom, and this leads to the feeling that it is appropriate to use containers and plant material associated with water. A lavabo, the utensil used by a priest for washing his hands during Mass, has come to be known as a decorative wall decoration. One of these, fastened to the wall, the basin filled with ferns, would be lovely, and ferns are not only associated with water because they are often found beside pools or in rain forests, but they thrive in a damp humid atmosphere. You could fasten a glass shelf to the wall and have a collection of ivies rooted in water in glass tumblers to match the color of your towels.

You might want to pick up the main color in your decorative scheme with a bouquet of flowers in an antique shaving mug on the counter—bachelor's buttons for blue, chrysanthemums or marigolds for yellow, and rambler roses for pink. In the winter, when there are no garden flowers, you could use the same idea with dried statice which comes in blue, yellow, and pink.

On a windowsill you could have a plant in a bottle, using one plant with a definite form rooted in water, the roots hidden by colored sea glass or glass pebbles. The bottle originally could have held bath salts. In a pastel-colored metal box that once held bath powder, you could have a bouquet of pink and lavender clover and daisies.

One woman had a most original idea for her bathroom decoration. Knowing that African violets grow well in a humid atmosphere, she turned the top of the toilet tank (which was under a window with good light) upside down and filled it with pebbles. On these she has pots of African violets. They thrive in the light and humidity and are usually a mass of blossoms.

4
Arrangements for Occasions and Holidays

Party Arrangements

Birthdays

Next to Christmas the most important day in a child's life is his birthday. And a birthday is a special day for any person whether he admits his age or not. An older person may protest that his should be ignored, but secretly he would be pleased for it to be a "party" day.

One charming birthday custom was brought back to this country by a man who was a major with our military government in Germany after World War II. One day, walking through the bombed out town where he was stationed, he felt sad. It was his birthday and he was a long way from his wife and children in America. The ruins in the town and the unhappy people didn't help his feeling of depression. He walked wearily into the dining room where his fellow officers were gathered for dinner and noticed that his chair was missing from the table. As he started to look around for another, the door flew open and in came two laughing maids carrying his chair. One cried "Happy Birthday" as they put the chair at his place. And what a chair it was. It was completely outlined with flowers.

The two maids were Lithuanian, and when by chance they found out about the major's birthday, they thought they would surprise him with one of the birthday customs of their country. They went into the fields and gathered flowers and leaves and fashioned garlands. These they fastened to the back of the chair, around the rungs, the seat, and legs of the chair until it looked as though it was made of flowers instead of wood. This thoughtful attention couldn't have come at a more welcome time, and the major was so pleased and impressed that he brought back the idea; now many of his friends use the Lithuanian custom for birthdays in their own families.

This arrangement for her mother's birthday party was made by an eight-year-old junior-garden-club member—an excellent example of the work youngsters are capable of doing. *Photo by Roche.*

Flower garlands like those used on the chair are easy to make.
1. Gather the flowers you want to use the day before, and condition them (see page 16 for details). Some of the sturdier wildflowers are useful—daisies, black-eyed Susans, Queen Anne's lace, cedar, huckleberry, and wild catbrier.
2. Make little bunches of flowers with stems two or three inches long, and wire the stems together or tie them with strong string. As you make each bunch, put it in water until you use it.
3. When you have all the material assembled, fasten an end of heavy green twine or cotton rope to a doorknob or drawer handle to hold it taut while you are working.
4. Start wiring the bunches on the twine, making sure that the flowers overlap and the stems don't show. Wind round and round continuously with the spool of wire.
5. Put a little bunch of greens between every three or four bunches of flowers.

Leis

We all know the lovely Hawaiian custom of greeting people with leis —garlands of flowers like a long necklace. In the South you can find the same material which these are made of in Hawaii—frangipani, plumeria, ginger, gardenias, and tiny orchids. In the North there are other flowers equally lovely for making a lei for someone to wear on a birthday, wedding anniversary, or other special occasion. Use round flowers like carnations, geraniums, daisies, zinnias, or chrysanthemums. Cut them close to the flower head, and with heavy thread and a large needle, string them as you would beads, pushing each flower tightly against the one preceding it. To keep the lei fresh, put it in a box lined with waxed paper, sprinkle it with water, and put it either in the refrigerator or in a plastic bag with a little water sprinkled in it and store in a cool place.

Decorating a Cake with Flowers

A birthday party wouldn't be complete without a cake, and a lovely way to decorate it is with flowers. Use one that was baked in a pan with a hole in the middle like an angel cake pan. Put a small glass in the hole, and make a nosegay in the glass for the center of the cake. Make a wreath of flower heads and greens around the bottom of the cake on the plate or tray.

Some children (with a little help from their mother) planned a novel cake for their grandmother. Supper was an outdoor barbecue, and when it came time for dessert, everyone went into the dining room. A green garland of smilax wound the length of the table, and nestled among the greens were sixty cupcakes, each with a lighted candle.

One of my young friends announced her engagement in an original way at a dinner party. For dessert, paper cups the proper size were filled with a delicious mousse and placed in ordinary flowerpots. The top of the mousse was sprinkled with powdered chocolate to look like dirt. A lovely rose with its foliage was stuck in the pot as though it was growing there, and garden tags were fastened to the roses. The names of the couple were written on the tags. The exclamations that greeted them were partly in surprise at the announcement and partly for the pretty effect of the pots of roses.

Engagement Parties

Showers for engaged couples seem more imaginative these days. One of the popular ones is a wine shower. For the buffet table at such a party, green wine bottles could be the containers. Put them on graduated boards and make line arrangements of grape ivy or ivy geranium foliage in them. Fasten bunches of grapes to florists' picks, and have them spilling from the necks of the bottles; arrange other bunches on the boards. Of course, if it is the proper season, it would be ideal to use natural grapevine with vine-ripened grapes.

Or, if a wooden wine rack is to be one of the gifts, put it in the center of the table, trail vines across it (fastened with Stickum), and have bunches of grapes spilling out of openings in the rack. Make the effect lush, with the feeling of a vineyard. With this you could use straw-covered wine bottles as candlesticks.

Another popular affair is a recipe shower. Each guest brings a favorite recipe typed on a file card, and a gift of whatever helps make the dish special—the type of pan needed to cook it, a can of an expensive ingredient, and so on. For the buffet arrangement here, a bouquet of herbs—artemisia, sage, rosemary, thyme, and mint—in a casserole dish would carry out the theme of the party.

For a bridesmaids' luncheon, the table should look as pretty and feminine as possible. Use your daintiest linen, thinnest glassware, and prettiest china. You could have a cloth the color of the bridesmaids' dresses and, for a centerpiece, miniature replicas of their bouquets set in the glass bowls that fit into candlesticks. Or you could borrow the idea of an old-fashioned Jack Horner pie for a centerpiece. Make an arrangement in the middle of the table with sentimental flowers like forget-me-nots, bleeding hearts, pansies, and lilies of the valley, and have a ribbon lead from the arrangement to each place. At the end of the ribbon, place the present from the bride to the bridesmaid, prettily wrapped, with a spray of flowers tied in the bow.

Anniversary Party

Since there are symbols for each wedding anniversary, it is easy to use this symbol in the decorating scheme for an anniversary party. For instance, the symbol for a tenth anniversary is tin. I attended a tenth-anniversary party—a large dinner party given at a club. In advance, friends saved tin fruit-juice cans, soup cans, and small ones like tuna-fish cans. The night of the party, the tin fruit-juice cans, placed at intervals on the long tables, held bouquets of flowers. Between them were the soup cans filled with Oasis, holding a candle in the middle with flowers around its base; the small cans served as ashtrays and nut dishes.

A ruby is the symbol for a fortieth anniversary, and if one happens to fall in June, what would be prettier on the party tables than clusters of red rambler roses arranged in coffee cans (which had been painted white and stippled with silver) between silver candlesticks?

Gifts

For an especially thoughtful gift, something associated with flowers is often the answer. Sometimes it is hard to find just the right note to say thank you to a hostess. Perhaps you don't want to give a conventional wedding gift. Maybe you want to give something that is uniquely for a certain person.

Recently, after a wonderful visit in Bermuda, I wanted to send my hostess something meaningful. Nothing from a shop seemed just right. Suddenly I had an idea. I had collected pods and cones while I was there, and so I made a Christmas pine-and-cone wreath using material from their house and ours. From their house were casuarina cones, false Indian almond, pods from Dutchman's pipe, and rattail cones. From our house were Japanese black pinecones, mallow pods, milkweed pods, lily pods, dock, and some fascinating clusters from our roadside that I still can't name. The card read, "Everything on the wreath grew within a hundred yards of your house or mine." I have never had a more enthusiastic thank-you note.

I know of a flower arranger, who, at the time of a wedding, finds out from the bride's mother where in her house she would like an arrangement. (Even if the wedding is not to be at home, there are always festivities connected with it.) Then she selects a container that is suitable for the desired spot, makes an arrangement in it, and gives the container to the bride for a wedding present.

If your wedding present to a bride is one that can hold flowers, you can have an arrangement in it that will add decoration to the display of wedding gifts. You might fill a brass planter with white geraniums, or an antique glass spoon holder with a bouquet of lilies of the valley. Another charming present that pleases a bride is a pair of framed arrangements of dried or pressed flowers. It is fairly easy to find attractive old frames at auctions or in secondhand or antique shops. If you buy these when you see them, and have a supply of pressed flowers on hand, you will never be at a loss for a present.

Perhaps you have a friend who loved to walk in the woods but is no longer able to do so because of health reasons. In the spring, why not make a little *dish garden,* using a shallow container of tiny wild plants —wild geranium, hepaticas, violets, and spring beauties? If you plant them when they are tiny, they will continue to grow and delight your friend for many days.

A *miniature* arrangement proved to be a perfect Christmas gift for a youngster to give her aunt, who collects miniature furniture. She found a discarded individual salt shaker, whose top was in perfect scale with the rest of the furniture. She used this as a container for tiny material like the tip of dried artemisia and baby's breath, sticking the material in the holes in the shaker top. It was perfect for the miniature dining table.

Corsages

The arrival of a shiny white square box from a florist containing a *corsage* is one of the big thrills of a girl's first dance. However, a homemade corsage is often the answer for a small gift. My memories of Easter as a child include, along with jelly-bean hunts and the smell of the black-dyed cotton of my choir robe, the little corsages of yellow daisies and bachelor's buttons that our mother always made for my sister and me to wear with our blue serge coats and leghorn hats to Sunday school.

On someone's birthday, a corsage to wear during the festivities makes a person of any age feel "special." It makes a nice way to welcome a guest of honor. Just recently I was with a group of young women who were making small corsages for the new mothers at the first PTA meeting of the year—a gracious welcoming gesture and at the same time a way of identifying those who were attending for the first time.

A small corsage makes an unusual and pretty way to decorate special packages. It also makes a festive party favor—for example, you could use a single large chrysanthemum and some autumn leaves as favors at a football luncheon.

Once you master a few little tricks of construction, corsages are not a bit hard to make. As for a flower arrangement, you start by conditioning the material you will use. You will need scissors, 22- and 24-gauge wire, florists' tape, and ribbon.

1. Cut the stem of a flower with a large calyx as near to the calyx as possible. If you want to make doubly sure of the flower's staying fresh, put a tiny piece of wet cotton over the cut stem end.
2. Take a piece of wire about eight inches long, and run it through

the bottom of the calyx near the stem so that it extends equally on each side. Bring these ends down and twist them together to make a "stem." In the case of a flower without a prominent calyx, and with a flat head like a daisy, push the piece of wire up through the center of the flower, then bend it down and push it through the center again, and twist it on the other end of the wire. It will be strong and pliable.

3. Then pinch the end of a piece of floral tape firmly around the top of the stem and hold it there in your left hand.
4. With your right hand twirl the tape around the wire stem.
5. Wire leaves by threading the wire through the base of the leaf with the finer wire. Wind these pieces of wire with tape also.
6. Assemble the flowers and leaves in the design you want, and join the wire stems by twisting them together. A ribbon is attractive but should be subordinate to the flowers.

A corsage shown with component parts—long wire to act as stems, one flower wired, one in the process of the wire stem being taped, and ribbon looped and wired into a bow. *Photo by Denby Versfeld Associates.*

**Other
Gift
Ideas**

Gather autumn leaves in the fall, and press them to keep for decorating gift packages. You can use ordinary brown wrapping paper and make the box gay with a sprinkling of these leaves glued on; and packages wrapped in yellow-, green-, orange-, or red-glazed paper are stunning with a scattering of these leaves.

An enchanting gift for someone who loves a garden, and which is reminiscent of our grandmothers' linen cupboards, is a jar of *potpourri*. This is made from a combination of flower petals and spices, whose scent can fill a room, a closet, or a bureau drawer.

To make potpourri: Gather flower petals from your garden that are just at the peak of their bloom. Because you want them to dry thoroughly, pick them when it hasn't rained for twenty-four hours and when they are not covered with dew. Since you want them for their fragrance, pick sweet-smelling flowers like mock orange, violets, heliotrope, verbena, and pinks. Rose petals should be dominant, so gather lots of them and remember that some of the new hybrid roses are not as fragrant as the more common roses.

There are several ways of drying the petals. You can spread them on absorbent paper towels on a flat surface in an airy room, or put them on a wire screen or hardware cloth so that air circulates around them. Or you can spread them in the sun in a sheltered spot.

Whatever method you use, when they are perfectly dry they are ready to mix with other ingredients. To four quarts of rose petals, add a handful of petals from other fragrant flowers and a half handful each of the minced leaves of herbs like mint, rosemary, bay leaf, or marjoram. There are many old and favorite recipes for adding spices and oils. Here is what you'll need:

    1 pound table salt
    ½ ounce storax
    1 ounce oil of bergamot
    ½ ounce orrisroot
    ½ teaspoon allspice
    1 ounce powdered cloves.

Mix all this together. Put the flowers and the spice mixture in alternate layers in a crock, stir them well, and cover tightly. When the mixture is well blended, put it into other small containers—small apothecary jars, empty bath-salts bottles, spice bottles, or any others that are suitable.

ᕽHalloween

Halloween means jack-o'-lanterns, trick-or-treating, and the combination of orange and black colors.

It isn't only children who like to make jack-o'-lanterns. Teenagers and grown-ups also like to carve pumpkins into grinning or grotesque faces, sometimes with appendages like green-pepper ears and carrot noses. Usually these are placed at the front door, but why not put them other places too? Try putting one on your lantern or fence post. Or make a nice big cheerful one and put it, lighted, in a prominent window in a darkened room. Or put a lighted one in the fireplace opening.

For a buffet table, you could fasten small jack-o'-lanterns to the candle cups of a black wrought-iron candelabrum and have lighted candles inside. Or for another centerpiece, a combination of orange flowers like calendulas, marigolds, and cockscomb with orange-striped croton in a black container would be seasonal.

"Ghost" Tree

A "ghost" tree makes an amusing arrangement for a hall table. To make this you will need a bare twiggy branch, or piece of driftwood as grotesquely shaped as possible, some Kleenex, some small rubber bands, and a black marking pen.

1. Put a pinholder on a base, and fasten the branch in it. (If it is heavy, you will find how to do this in the section on Mechanical Aids.)
2. On the tip of each twig or subsidiary branch, stick a piece of plant material that will give a weird effect. My favorites are the slender,

pointed red and green peppers that are available in the market at this season and are twisted into fantastic shapes, but you could also use string beans, brussels sprouts, radishes with roots, or sprouted onions.

3. Make some ghosts to perch on the tree by rolling a piece of Kleenex into a ball. Place the center of another piece of Kleenex around the ball, and fasten it with a rubber band. This makes the head, and the rest of the second piece of Kleenex billows out to form a robe.

4. With a black Magic Marker draw a grotesque face on the head. Make enough ghosts to perch on the tree and on the board at the base.

This "arrangement" never fails to amuse those who see it. In fact it is done in the foyer of our Yacht Club each Halloween by popular request.

You can surprise favorite neighbors by ringing their doorbells on trick-or-treat night and leaving small hollowed-out pumpkins filled with small chrysanthemums, goldenrod, wild asters, and autumn leaves.

Thanksgiving

Autumn is a time of blazing color, crisp invigorating air, and an abundance of Nature's bounty. Roadside stands are piled high with harvest fruits and vegetables, hard-shelled nuts fall to the ground in wooded groves, and country lanes are fragrant with the winy smell of wild grapes warmed in the sun. And just as the Pilgrims gathered three hundred years ago to give thanks for their first harvest, it is a time for family reunions at Thanksgiving.

Centerpieces

Brilliant leaves, the last garden flowers, fruits, nuts, and vegetables make the most appropriate and beautiful decorations for these festive Thanksgiving tables. Visit a roadside stand, and arrangements for centerpieces will suggest themselves. A large silvery boat-shaped Hubbard squash can be hollowed out and used as a container. It can be filled with the dark green acorn squash, green apples, red cabbage, purple cauliflower, and purple vine-ripened grapes displayed around it on the stand. A red cabbage makes a beautiful flower form when the outside leaves are curled back. This, as well as acorn squash, can be impaled on long sticks to anchor them in an arrangement.

Perhaps your china is gold and white, and you are using a heavy white linen or damask cloth. Why not use a garland as a centerpiece? This is especially good for a large family table, as the decoration is low enough not to interfere with any cross-table conversation. You can arrange flat magnolia or rhododendron leaves in a garland pattern, or you can take cuttings of ilex or boxwood and place them on the table so that they make a thick garland about five inches wide, or you can buy smilax roping from a florist. On the garland, place clusters of fruit at intervals, choosing those that are predominantly yellow or gold—kumquats, Seckel pears, mandarins, tiny gourds, lemons—with clusters of cranberries for accent.

Another way to use fruit or vegetables in a flat arrangement, is to cut a Styrofoam wreath in half. Put the two halves in the center of the table in an S shape or reverse curve, and cover it with greens and fruit and/or vegetables.

Because of its association with harvest time the cornucopia, or "horn of plenty," is a suitable container for Thanksgiving. These are sold widely and for an informal table can be used in the natural straw in which they are usually made, or you can spray them gold or silver. They are usually placed horizontally on the table and filled with fruit arranged so that some is spilling out on the table. If you use one in the natural straw it is nice to include wheat in the arrangement, not only because it relates in color and texture but because it is appropriate to the season. If you use it, wire it in sprays to florist picks. It is more effective used that way rather than individual stalks. For the more formal table, the fruit would be luxurious—large perfect peaches, huge hothouse grapes, apples with beautiful color and satiny sheen.

If you are lucky enough to have a silver epergne, the kind with a center container and smaller ones branching from it, this is the perfect time to use it. You can have either flowers or fruit in the center opening, and make miniature fruit or flower arrangements in the lower ones. A combination of fruit and flowers is attractive in these arrangements. The fruits in the lower arrangements should be small in scale, and the lovely fall berries like viburnum, fire thorn, or pokeweed would fit in here.

Place Cards

It is fun to have place cards for special dinners, and making them can be a fine family project. For Thanksgiving, try gluing tiny pieces of corn husk or dried grass stalks in the typical pyramid of corn shocks to small rectangular pieces of cardboard. At the base of the miniature corn shocks, glue orange fire-thorn berries to look like pumpkins.

Or you can cut a piece of heavy metallic gold, silver, or copper foil in the shape of a tiny compote, and make a tiny fruit arrangement on it. You can glue on red berries for apples, purple privet berries for grapes, and seeds for nuts.

**Decorating
Your
Door**

People are no longer limiting their hospitality to dinners at Thanksgiving. More and more you are seeing doors decorated. This is a lovely custom, for it is a way of saying "Welcome" at a joyous season.

Instead of hanging a few ears of Indian corn, however, why not go a step further and make a swag? By using a block of Styrofoam for a base, this is really quite simple. The size block you need depends on the finished size you want. For one that is about three feet from top to bottom, you would need a piece about six by four inches and two inches thick. Wrap two pieces of strong wire around the block, one horizontally and one vertically, fastening the two ends together in the back to form a loop for hanging.

It is easiest to make the swag in place right on the door. In this way you keep the design in proportion to the background as you work. Unless you are using material with a very stiff stem, wire each piece of material to a florists' pick so that you can stick it in the Styrofoam block. If you do this securely, the wind and opening or closing the door will not disturb it.

There is a wealth of material to use at this season. What you choose depends on the color of the door, for the swag will have this as a background. If the color is green or brown, it is a perfect background for a swag made of dried material ranging from golden beige to dark brown. There are wheat, sea oats, dried okra, various palms, dock, cattails, croton, and yucca pods, to name but a few.

Establish the top, bottom, and outer edges of the design with some of the spiky, lighter-colored material and work toward the middle, · solidifying the outside lines with some of the darker slender material. Work toward a focal point in the center with other interesting forms. You can have a ribbon bow or one made from natural material—ribbon grass, corn husks that have been soaked until they are pliable, bent rattail cones, or boiled locust pods. Bend this natural material into loops, wire it into the size bow you wish, and stick it into the Styrofoam with a florists' pick.

If your door is white, use some of the colorful dried material like orange lantern plant, yellow yarrow, and mother-of-pearl honesty.

You can make a swag that features a pineapple, the symbol of hospitality. In order to anchor the pineapple firmly at the focal point, use a rectangle of hardware cloth (described in the section on Mechanical Aids) so that you can put wires through the center of the pineapple as well as the top and bottom, in order to wire it firmly to the hardware cloth. Then wire a piece of Styrofoam to the hardware cloth. This will make the pineapple stand away from the door and permit you to insert other material into the hardware cloth and the Styrofoam. You can use either dried material or greens for the swag, but it is attractive to use fruits or vegetables like small artichokes, tiny scrubbed potatoes, pomegranates, and yellow apples around the focal pineapple.

A unique door decoration uses an Osage orange for the center. Osage oranges are the large yellowish-green fruits of the maclura tree which is native in many of our states. The fruit probably got its name because the tree was a favorite of the Osage Indians who used the wood for making bows. The fruit is inedible but is filled with a milklike fluid which keeps stems fresh when they are thrust in it. Using the orange as the center, make a green wreath around it by sticking pieces of ilex or boxwood or other evergreen foliage directly into the fruit. Make a circle of color around the green orange with sprays of orange fire thorn or other berries. To prepare it for hanging, put a piece of very heavy wire, or a skewer, through the wreath from top to bottom. Make a loop at the top, and fasten pieces of green and colored velvet ribbon to the loop, tie the ends in a bow, and hang it on the door.

If you don't want a decoration on the door, how about the *doorstep?* It could be as formal as a garden urn filled with chrysanthemums, or as simple as a wooden scrap basket filled with autumn leaves, or a wooden trough filled with small pumpkins, colorful squash, gourds, and Indian corn.

Christmas

Christmas to us is a festival to celebrate the birth of Christ, but long before Christ was born, pagan people worshiped the sun and held celebrations at this time of year to mark the Winter Solstice—the time that the sun starts its course back toward earth from the farthest place from the equator. And strange as it may seem, many of the customs we use at Christmas stem from this heathen civilization. These primitive people used evergreen garlands and wreaths. They believed that the round wreath was a symbol of eternity and that evergreen branches were a symbol of eternal life. Holly, ivy, and mistletoe were favored because they were not only green but bore berries in winter. The ancient kissing bough was a forerunner of our Christmas tree. To these ancient customs we have added those we associate with Christ's birth—crèches, gifts, carols, stars, and angels. We have also adopted Christmas customs from other countries—carol singing from Germany, lighting of candles from Scandinavian countries, and Yule logs and plum puddings from England. All of these traditions combine to make Christmas one of the merriest times of the year and one of the most spiritual.

Is there anything more fun to do at Christmastime than to go foraging for greens and other plant material to make your own decorations? Whether you are crunching through the snow in a New England pine forest, cutting blazing poinsettias in Florida, gathering myriads of beautiful pinecones in California, or picking luxuriant holly in the Pacific Northwest, there is something about assembling your own decorations that is smugly satisfying.

In the area where I live, there is the combination of seashore and lovely holly trees that to me is thrilling. Recently, on a day when the snowy ground and the brilliant blue sky seemed to vie to see which could sparkle the most, I gathered armfuls of holly from tall trees which stood on the bank of a river in view of the ocean. I loved it.

There are three basic decorations that most of us picture when we think of Christmas—a wreath, a garland or swag, and a Christmas tree. Let's talk about ways to make and use them.

Wreaths

A bushy green wreath, tied with a bright red bow, is lovely in its own fragrant simplicity. I will never forget a square white Colonial house on a snowy New England hillside I saw one Christmas Eve. The front of the house was floodlit, and on the outside of every window was a green pine wreath with a big red bow.

It is easy to make a wreath of greens. First you need a circular *foundation:*

1. Cut pliable wands of shrubs like privet or forsythia.
2. Reinforce the circle by twisting more of the pliable material over and around it.
3. Fasten the ends by weaving into the basic circle.

Another way of making a foundation is to bend a coat hanger into proper shape, leaving the hook to hang the wreath. If you do this, wind the wire with masking tape to make the surface less slippery.

If you don't want to go to the trouble of making your own foundation, you can buy wire foundation hoops at florists, or ones made of straw and other materials at hobby shops.

Once you have your foundation, here's how to make the *wreath:*

1. Gather evergreens and cut them into four- or five-inch pieces.
2. Wire these into little bunches, using four or five pieces for each bunch. You can use the same kind of greens, or combine several varieties.
3. When you have a number of bunches prepared, take a spool of fairly heavy wire and wire each bunch on the hoop, all in the same direction, turning the spool round and round the wreath in a continuous line.

You can make these wreaths well in advance of Christmas. *To store,* put them in plastic bags and keep them in a cool place, even outdoors.

There are many ways to *decorate* a plain green wreath. One way is to make a Della Robbia design patterned after the enamel-covered terra-cotta fruit made famous by the Florentine Della Robbia family. For an outdoor wreath of this kind, it is best to use artificial fruit and waterproof ribbon so that it will look fresh in any kind of weather. It

Many kinds of pine cones and seedpods make an interesting and attractive wreath as described in the text on page 164. Wreath arranged by Katherine N. Cutler.

can be bright or muted. A bright wreath would use small bunches of grapes of different colors, small lemons, walnuts, lady apples, limes, and cones, with a big rosette bow of red ribbon, lined with green and ending in streamers.

If your door is protected from the weather by a vestibule, it is fun to make a wreath with real fruit, perhaps in more muted colors. Use evergreens that have more gray tones than bright pine has. Instead of a whole circle of artificial fruit you can use clusters of real fruit—lady apples, bronze Seckel pears, yellow-red love apples (solanum), grayblue juniper berries, and green grapes. A moss-green velvet bow would be pretty with this.

Fruits that are good to use for Della Robbia wreaths are lady apples, crab apples, lemons, limes, kumquats, cranberries, nuts, tangerines, mandarins, Seckel pears, and small pinecones.

Plant material can be used on green wreaths to emphasize a color scheme. I am thinking of a doorway that has two lovely amber glass-paneled lanterns on each side. At Christmas a green pine wreath is hung under each lantern, tied with bows of velvet ribbon the same golden yellow as the amber glass, and decorated with pinecones dusted with gold.

You might want to decorate a wreath over a fireplace to emphasize unusual colors in your living room. One such that I saw, in a room with yellow walls and colors in the room of a rosy rust and moss green, was decorated with bunches of artificial Tokay grapes, and cones, sweet gum balls, and acorns that had all been picked at an early stage of growth when they were moss green. Hung over the fireplace, the wreath tied all the colors in the room together.

A circle of gilded nuts against a green wreath has a feeling of restrained elegance. Clusters of silver bells wired on florists' picks in clusters around a wreath, with a bow made from a string of sleigh bells, gives a musical as well as fragrant welcome.

Asparagus Sprengeri fern, which grows profusely in warm climates, makes lovely Christmas wreaths. The small feathery leaves grow on long pliant stems that are easy to bind together in a circle. To make the wreath full, wire several circles together. An effective way to decorate such a wreath is to fasten wire around real or artificial clusters of red berries, and thrust the wire into the center of green pittosporum rosettes, making dark green flowers with red centers. Or you can wire green and red croton leaves in bowlike shapes.

Another kind of wreath that is fascinating to make is one of pinecones, nuts, and seedpods like the one shown on page 163. These are perhaps the most fun of all to create. First of all there is the excitement of finding unusual material. You can be on the lookout all year for different-shaped pods, cones, and dried material that would be pretty in your Christmas wreath. I have already discussed, in the section on Collecting, the circumstances under which I have acquired material. Also, if your friends know that you enjoy making such wreaths, they will send you surprises. I have been sent cocoanut calyxes from Florida, wood roses from Hawaii, cones from California, and dried okra pods from Texas, in addition to the ones I found myself.

To make these wreaths, you will need a wide circle of Masonite, wall board, or similar material, a can of linoleum paste—the kind used for laying a linoleum floor—and a wide putty knife to spread the paste. If you don't want to cut the foundation circle yourself, you can have it done at a lumberyard. Assemble all of your material on a newspaper-covered table. Fasten a wire loop around the top of the wreath to hang it. Spread paste generously on each area as you work. (It will feel as though you are lavishly icing a cake with frosting of just the right consistency.)

As in any flower arrangement, plan a design. You will first need to give a finished effect to the inner and outer edges of the circle. Individual petals cut from large California cones pressed close together in the paste with the rounded side out will give a scalloped effect. (You can buy these at a florist's if you don't have any. One or two of these huge cones will yield a quantity of petals.) You can use tiny casuarina cones, matched in size for the border, or almonds with the pointed end out.

When the inner and outer edges are complete, make a focal point or center of interest at the top of the wreath, and another at the bottom. For good balance, the one at the bottom should be larger in area. Use some of the larger more interesting shapes for these like wood roses, deodar cones, cocoanut calyxes, or pinecones cut in half. Next, make small centers of interest on each side of the wreath. Then, to lead your eye around the circle, use curved material like curved pods, cones, or rattail cones between the centers of interest. Now you have established the basic design, and you can fill in solidly with the rest of the material.

Use plenty of paste, smearing it on thickly. The nice thing about linoleum paste is that, although eventually it gets completely hard, it takes several hours so that if you want to make changes in the design after you complete the wreath, you can.

When the wreath is finished, you can either leave it in its natural shades of brown coloring, or you can dust it with silver or gold, or spray it solidly with those colors. It is effective by itself, tied with a two-toned green and brown or gold or silver bow, or you can fasten it to a larger green wreath, where it makes a striking circle against the dark green background.

Making these wreaths is so engrossing that onlookers want to get into the act. Once a doctor neighbor, who was having a well-earned pre-Christmas vacation, came by as I was working on one. He said, "That looks like fun. I'm going to make a 'beachcomber's wreath.'" He went for a walk on the beach and gathered his material. He came back with mussel shells, crab claws, bits of sea glass, bits of cork, a fish lure, clamshells of various sizes, little pieces of curvy wood, cat's-eye shells, and some mallow pods and dried goldenrod he had picked up on the path to the beach. He made his wreath, following the design of my wreath, and what had started out as a tongue-in-cheek joke turned out to be perfectly beautiful. When he sprayed it heavily with gold, it was a fascinating study in texture since some of the material was very smooth and the rest, rough. His wife hung it against a green wreath, and it was a conversation piece for the balance of the holidays.

Swags and Garlands

If, instead of a wreath on your door, you want a *swag,* you can make one by the same method described in the chapter on Thanksgiving. You can also use heavy pine branches wired together. A simple but distinctive swag for a Christmas door is to wire together two large curving pine branches like white pine. In the center, fasten three huge "sleigh bells" made by cutting their conventional slotted openings in Styrofoam balls and then spraying the balls silver. If you want color on such a swag instead, use artificial poinsettias or a cluster of bright fruit in the center.

Roping for *garlands* is not hard to make. Do be careful, though, not to use conservation material like prince's pine, which, though tempting because of its formation, is becoming all too scarce. Also, while hemlock is pretty used in combination with other greens, it drops more quickly than some of the other evergreens and so is not as satisfactory to use for a whole garland. Broad-leafed evergreens like laurel are pretty used alone or in combination with long-needled material.

To Make a Garland

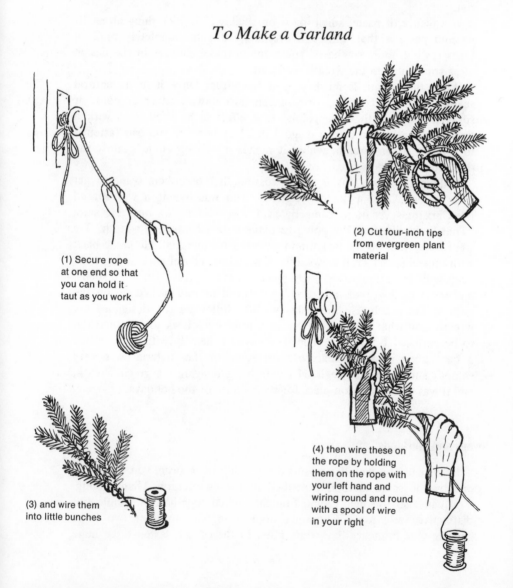

(1) Secure rope at one end so that you can hold it taut as you work

(2) Cut four-inch tips from evergreen plant material

(3) and wire them into little bunches

(4) then wire these on the rope by holding them on the rope with your left hand and wiring round and round with a spool of wire in your right

For a foundation use several strands of twine wound together, or heavy cotton rope.

For old-fashioned garlands and swags we usually use the so-called Christmas greens like pine, cedar, and spruce—but there are many others that are suitable. Laurel, rhododendron, magnolia, euonymous, and ivy are smooth and green. For color there is variegated ivy, yellow and white variegated holly, yellow variegated euonymous, blue-gray Atlantic cedar (*Cedrus atlantica*), and the browns of glycerin-treated foliage.

Green roping is lovely festooned on the stairway, wound on banisters, draped on fireplaces or over doorways. It can be trimmed like wreaths in the Della Robbia manner with fruit or with gilded cones, nuts, real flowers in water picks, or gay ribbons.

If you want a shaped or stylized garland for your fireplace, you can cut a background shape from hardware cloth and cover it with greens and other decorative material.

Christmas Trees

Probably the one decoration that says Christmas to everyone is the Christmas tree. The tree is the center of festivity throughout the holiday season. Each family has its own traditional way of trimming it, and woe to the ones who try to make them change. I have heard it said that this can be a conflict between brides and grooms in the first year of their marriage.

There are other ways of using a Christmas tree in addition to having it the main feature. One of my favorites is the flat tree illustrated here. To make the foundation, take a piece of thin metal or heavy wire and bend it into a triangular shape, bringing the ends together at the base and widening them out again to make a simulated tub. Cover the triangular frame with chicken wire, bending the cut edges around the frame. Fasten a piece of thick branch between the "tree" and the base to form a trunk.

Weave evergreen tips about five inches long into the chicken wire until you have a solid, bushy flat tree. When you make the cuttings, try to use ones with pointed ends, and use these for the outside edges. It is easiest to put in the top point first, and then two symmetrical pointed pieces for the bottom sides. In this way you establish the triangular design in the beginning. Cover the base with cardboard, thin wood, foil, or whatever will be best with your decoration.

These trees hang flat and can be used on a door, or put on the wall over a mantel. One woman endeared herself to all the neighborhood

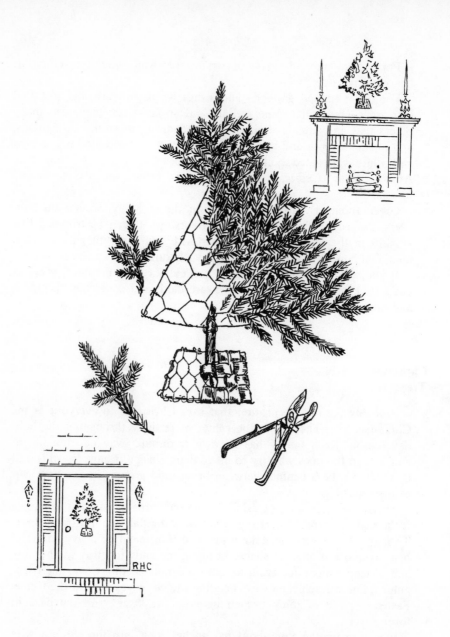

children with one of these trees. She made dozens of little popcorn balls and wrapped them in red cellophane. She hung one of the trees on her front door and decorated it with the popcorn balls stuck into the tree with florists' picks. The finishing touch was a big red bow tied around the trunk of the tree, from which hung streamers of red ribbon and little bells. It was soon noised around the neighborhood that the children were welcome to help themselves to the popcorn balls. When she heard the bells tinkling, this woman knew the time had come to replace balls on the tree with those she kept ready in a bowl in the hallway.

Another charming way to decorate one of these trees for a doorway is to put a sprig of holly loaded with red berries in the center, and fasten miniature red birds to the tree to look as though, attracted by the berries, they had paused in flight.

You could hang one of these over a mantel and decorate it with fresh flowers in water picks. Paper-white narcissus, white freesia, pink or red carnations all last well.

Imaginative Ideas
for Christmas

Sometimes the simplest decorations are the loveliest. We visited a house one Christmas where this was true. The family had moved in just before the holidays, and the house needed to be completely redecorated inside. Instead of fretting that the background wasn't just the way she wanted it for her usual distinctive decorations, the mother engineered a "greens-gathering day." Equipped with thermos bottles of hot soup and a basket of hearty sandwiches, the whole family went tramping through the New England woods and fields collecting many seedling evergreen trees about two feet high. Back home they put the trees in pots, tied a big saucy red bow on each, and put them all around the house—on tables, the hearth, stair landings, mantels, and wide windowsills. When you walked in the house and were greeted by the fragrance of the perky little trees with their festive red bows, you didn't notice the dingy wallpaper—you just thought, "Christmas is here."

For modern houses you can make a stylized Christmas tree by cutting a triangular shape from Masonite or wall board and decorating it in the same way as the pine and cone wreaths, using the same materials. For rooms in the neutral tones, used in these houses they look good left in the natural colors, although a light spraying of gold will give a Christmas sparkle.

And when we think of Christmas trees let's not forget the birds. You can trim an outdoor tree just for them. Make a star for the top by thickly coating a star-shaped wire frame with peanut butter and sticking popcorn in it. Make baskets from hollowed-out grapefruit and orange halves with wire handles, and fill them with bacon fat. Make balls of suet, raisins, and seeds, and wreaths of cranberries. Your decorations may not last long, but you'll have a wonderful time watching the birds enjoying them. If you live in an apartment, you can make a miniature tree for the birds. Get a large pinecone with open petals. Most florists sell these at Christmastime. Save things like bread and cracker crumbs, leftover cereal, broken nuts, melon seeds, and broken potato chips, and stir them into melted suet and bacon fat. When the mixture hardens, fill the crevices between the petals of the cone with it.

Table Settings
for Christmas

A beautifully decorated and appointed table sets the scene for festive dining. One centerpiece that would be elegant and distinctive uses green and gold fruit. Ideally the container would be a large compote. If you don't have an antique one, say white and gold, you can make a compote by fastening a round silver tray to a heavy silver candlestick with Stickum. Use a pineapple for height, and try to find one that is more green than brown, with a green top that curves. You can accent the curve by pulling out a few of the leaves (like shaping eyebrows). Use natural green limes and avocados, and spray the rest of the fruit you are using, including grapes, gold. When sprayed gold, the grainy texture of kumquats, tangerines, and oranges makes a pleasing contrast with the satiny appearance of the grapes, apples, and pears. Clusters of natural green laurel are tucked between the fruit. This arrangement, used on a soft green or white cloth with gold and white china, has great distinction. The sprayed fruit will last two weeks. This is an idea for someone who doesn't want to use red in her dining room.

For an informal table in an Early American-type house, there is another attractive way to use fruit. Have made at a lumberyard a wooden cone five and a half inches across the bottom and two and a half inches diameter at the top. Hammer nails with tiny heads in evenly spaced rows up and down and around, one half inch apart. The nail must be long enough to stick out a good half inch, and strong enough to support a heavy fruit without bending. Also the angle of the nail should be minimally "up." Stick shiny red apples on the nails, making a pyramid of fruit. Put clusters of greens, or little green velvet bows, between the apples. Put a wreath of greens around the base.

There is a pretty table decoration that children love to make at Christmas. Gather dried weeds and grasses from the fields and roadsides—dock, milkweed pods, dried Queen Anne's lace, dried goldenrod, in fact anything that is stiff and of an interesting shape. Spread them out on a piece of newspaper and spray them with silver paint. When they are dry, you can arrange them by sticking them in a ball of florists' clay. A little glitter sprinkled on them while they are wet adds a sparkly touch. You can paint the clay ball silver, too. This arrangement is lovely placed on a mirror, a silver tray, or a crystal container.

One Christmas dinner table that I will always remember was a truly family one. It was in a gracious New England dining room. There were eighteen people at the table, ranging in age from a ninety-year-old great-grandfather to a year-old baby in a high chair. There was a fire burning in the fireplace and huge snowflakes were falling outside the bowed window. The table was sophisticated in design for the adults and yet appealing to the children. The long table was covered with a white cloth. A wide red satin ribbon, with a not quite so wide green one on top of it, ran down the center of the table, hanging down to the edges of the cloth at each end. In the center was a handsome red and gold sleigh filled with holly and tiny gaily wrapped packages. It was driven by a jolly Santa Claus, brandishing a whip over six pair of white reindeer with red and gold harnesses.

Kitchens

Don't forget the kitchen at Christmas. Little Della Robbia wreaths for the windows would be charming made on a Styrofoam base with laurel leaves. If the Styrofoam wreath is too thick, cut it in half with a sharp knife. Wash the laurel leaves well and rub them to a gloss with waxed paper. Then pin overlapping leaves on the Styrofoam until it is well covered. Wire small artificial fruits into a little circle, and fasten it on the laurel wreath with small brads or hairpins.

A green wreath of fresh herbs stays fresh quite a long time, especially if you sprinkle it with a little water. The nice part is that you can let it dry in place and enjoy its spicy fragrance after Christmas is over.

Candles

We think of candlelight especially at Christmas. The warmth of its glow adds to the spirit of the holiday season. There are many ways to use candles other than the obvious ones.

An antique candle mold, backed by branches of evergreen sweeping high on one side and low on the other and filled with red candles graduated in size to follow the curve of the branches, would be a cheery greeting on a hall table. Always be particularly careful, though, when you combine evergreens with candles that the candles won't come in contact with the greens while lighted. There are fireproofing substances that you can use to treat greens to be doubly sure of safety.

The round Oasis holders mentioned in the Mechanical Aids chapter make ideal holders for greens and candles. A large round candle, about three inches in diameter, will fit in the inner circle. Secure it firmly

with Oasis. The outer circle can be packed with wet Oasis and made
into an arrangement around the base of the candle. An attractive one
would be the traditional holly and ivy, or you could use sprigs of evergreen with garnet roses or red carnations.

Three large round candles of different heights on a wooden lazy
Susan, their base surrounded with holly or evergreen, make a stunning
and easy-to-fix arrangement for a round pine table. In a more formal
house, you can have a large green candle in the middle of a gold pine-
and-pod wreath.

The tiny glasses holding food-warming candles, placed in a holly
wreath, would make a twinkling centerpiece.

**Kissing
Balls**

No house is quite complete at Christmas without a "kissing ball."
These hold a sprig of mistletoe and are hung from an inside doorframe
or chandelier. There are many legends surrounding the kissing ball,
some of them from pagan times. No two are alike, but it is agreed that
anyone standing under the mistletoe may be kissed.

One way to make these delightful ornaments:

1. Using two circles of an embroidery hoop, cover the hoops by
   winding them with ribbon. You can wind one with green ribbon
   and one with red. (A more elaborate way to decorate it is to sew
   pearls at intervals to red velvet ribbon and then glue this to the
   outside of the hoop with the green on the inside.)
2. When the hoops are covered, fit one inside the other so that they
   make a round cage to hold a little bouquet of mistletoe fastened,
   with a ribbon bow, to the top where the hoops cross.

Another Way to Make a Kissing Ball

1. Run a long meat skewer through a big apple.
2. Cover the apple completely, making a round ball by sticking pieces
   of a shiny evergreen like boxwood, ilex, or azalea into the apple.
   (The moisture will keep the greens fresh.)
3. Decorate by scattering tiny red bows over it, fastening them with
   pearl-headed corsage pins.
4. Fasten a cluster of mistletoe to the bottom of the ball by wiring
   it onto the exposed end of the skewer, making sure that the latter
   is covered.
5. Wire the top end of the skewer with narrow red ribbon ending in
   a bow with streamers. You can use the streamers to hang it.

Valentine's Day

Valentine's Day is a sentimental holiday. It brings to mind young lovers, red hearts, dainty lace, cupids, and old-fashioned flowers like bleeding hearts, pansies, forget-me-nots, rosebuds, mignonettes, and pinks. Old-fashioned containers like epergnes, cupids holding bowls like the one in the photo on page 174, and Victorian fan-shaped vases are suitable for these flowers.

Cloths for Valentine tables are of lace or fine linen in pastel shades. If you aren't the pastel type, you can have a striking table by using a red cloth. Cut various-sized hearts out of heavy red paper, and fasten a wire to each. Cover the wire with green floral tape. Now you have heart-shaped "flowers" and can make an arrangement of them with green foliage for the center of the table.

You can make Valentine topiary trees by fastening an apple on a slim green rod and sticking the rod in a lump of floral clay. Make a round "tree" in the apple by sticking snips of greens in it as you did for the kissing ball in the previous chapter. Scatter little red hearts over it, fastening each with a tiny piece of Stickum.

If someone sends you long-stemmed red roses for a valentine, be brave and cut the beautiful long stems into different lengths. I know it is something that one does reluctantly, but the finished arrangement will be so much prettier than if it is top-heavy with the roses all at the same level.

From your supply of pressed flowers you can make pretty valentines. One way is to cut a large heart from construction paper or cardboard. It need not be red. Sometimes it is pretty to have pink or white ones. On the heart make a design with pressed flowers and leaves. These should be tiny, like forget-me-nots, alyssum, ageratum, baby's breath, statice, et cetera. Use a small paintbrush or Q-Tip to touch the back of each with glue as you place them. You can form the flowers into a garland design following the heart shape, or you can make a wreath in the center with a little bow at the top. If the heart is red, you can cut edging from a lace-paper doily and paste it to the back of the heart so that it makes an outline around the edge. If the heart is pink or white, you can paste it to a larger heart cut from red cardboard or construction paper.

A sentimental arrangement of hearts and flowers. Roses and carnations are combined with passionflower vine and hearts strung on a wire in a container supported by dancing cupids.

Easter

Although Easter is essentially a religious holiday, it has also come to be a holiday that especially appeals to children and that adults enjoy because it heralds spring.

Children look forward to coloring Easter eggs, having jelly-bean hunts, and receiving presents of Easter baskets filled with candy, and toy rabbits and chickens. When children are dyeing eggs, have them do some for a table centerpiece. On a table, using a cream or yellow cloth, you could have a centerpiece of forsythia branches with yellow, brown, orange, and lavender eggs nestled beneath them—or a pink cloth with forced Japanese quince blossoms and pink, blue, and lavender eggs.

The children can make place cards for the table. Break off the tip of a raw egg, empty it, and when the shell is dry, paint it a color to match the centerpiece. Make stands for the eggshells by folding a heavy piece of paper and cutting a tiny semicircle at the fold for the eggshell to rest in. Fill the shell with a little nosegay, and put one at each place. Or they can fill the shell with dirt and plant a tiny plant in it. Later you can plant it in the garden, eggshell and all.

Other pretty Easter favors that children can make start with an empty spool. Paint the spool a nice color. Paste a piece of foil on the bottom, and stuff the hole with crumbled wet Oasis. Use grape hyacinths, violets, or sprigs of fruit blossoms stuck in the Oasis to simulate a little plant.

A very simple table arrangement, but one that could only mean Easter, would be to use a pretty round hatbox for a container. Put something inside to hold water, and fill it with flowers that are typically spring—daffodils, pussy willows, violets, or pansies.

If pastel colors don't suit your home, try making a naturalistic arrangement on a brown or green cloth, using gnarled bare branches with moss and small spring flowers like crocuses, violets, or scillas at the bottom. Put chocolate rabbits in various poses on the moss as though they were playing there.

Patriotic Occasions

Red, white, and blue is the obvious color combination for parties on Washington's Birthday, Lincoln's Birthday, Memorial Day, and the Fourth of July. There is a trick to using this combination, though. Using them in equal parts is weak and ineffective. It is much more dramatic to use one of the colors with white and employ the other as an accent.

For instance, you could have a red and white checked tablecloth, white plates, dark blue tumblers, and white pots of red geraniums for a centerpiece. Or you might have a dark blue cloth, white milk glass plates and tumblers, and a milk glass compote with bachelor's buttons, white feverfew, and a few red carnations.

It is fun to set a table in red, white, and blue because if you don't happen to own cloths, china, and glasses in these colors, there are many things to buy that are very inexpensive. You can get red-and-white- and blue-and-white-striped ticking and red-and-white- and blue-and-white-checked gingham for cloths. These are especially gay when bordered with white fringe. Hardware and variety stores carry inexpensive glass plates, tumblers, and goblets in dark blue and deep red and imitation milk glass.

If you don't want conventional containers for flowers, you can make symbolic ones—for example, you can make a drum by painting a coffee can white and stringing it with red and blue cord, gluing some of the cord around the edge. You can make firecrackers of all sizes by gluing Chinese-red paper to fruit-juice cans. It would even be fun on Lincoln's Birthday to make a little scene on the table, with pieces of pine for trees, a log cabin made with children's building logs, and a little garden (made from pieces of red geranium, individual florets of feverfew or delphinium, and bits of bachelor's button stuck in wet Oasis) around a flagpole flying a flag.

The cylinders of cardboard in the center of rolls of gift-wrapping paper painted red, and filled with dried goldenrod or similar material sprayed red and yellow, would simulate an exploding rocket for a hall table arrangement, or you might paint the rolls from inside toilet tissue silver and fill them with miniature cattails sprayed silver to simulate sparklers.

Red, white, and blue flowers suitable to use are:

Red	*White*	*Blue*
Anemone	Carnation	Anemone
Anthurium	Daisy	Bachelor's Button
Camellia	Feverfew	Delphinium
Carnation	Freesia	Grape Hyacinth
Cockscomb	Gladiolus	Iris
Geranium	Stock	Statice
Gladiolus	Sweet Pea	
Rose	Tulip	

5

Using Your Talents for Others

Oasis blocks fastened on brass candelabra held twin arrangements to complement central portrait in color and design. *Photo by Denby Versfeld Associates. Arrangement by Katherine N. Cutler.*

Stephanotis, miniature roses, and miniature carnations in an alabaster epergne make and arrangement in traditional tiered wedding cake design. *Photo by Denby Versfeld Associates. Arrangement by Katherine N. Cutler.*

The same eperge used for a Christmas arrangement, (inset). *Photo by Roche. Arrangement by Katherine N. Cutler.*

There is a tropical feeling in this setting for a terrace luncheon using a coconut spathe from Florida, orchids, coral and philodendron. *Photo by Roche. Arrangement by Katherine N. Cutler.*

This arrangement serves to tie the components of this table together. The flowers repeat the colors in the china and cloth, and the pewter container is related to the candelabrum, the salad bowl, and coffee service. *Lenox china courtesy of Jane Smith Shops. Arrangement by Katherine N. Cutler.*

Eighteenth-century-period arrangement of dried statice, dock, sage, daisies, and Queen Anne's lace. *Photo by Denby Versfeld Associates. Arrangement by Katherine N. Cutler.*

Church Flowers

In many churches the arrangement of flowers for the altar is left to a florist. There is nothing wrong with this, but the arrangements (usually done in the stereotyped altar vases) will have a sameness each Sunday, lightened only by different varieties of flowers. As more people are becoming interested in flower arrangement, this system is changing, and individuals are discovering that there are many different ways to use flowers in churches.

It is not uncommon now for a talented arranger to form a committee with other interested members of the congregation to arrange the flowers for church services. The flowers may still come from a florist, from members' gardens, or be wildflowers or foliage. Nothing is prohibited, and one of the nicest features is that material is now being used that formerly was not considered suitable. I was shocked once to hear a minister object to black-eyed Susans being used on the altar of his beautiful but simple white Colonial church. He said they weren't "nice enough." I mentally cheered when I heard the woman who was arranging them say, her own black eyes snapping, "God made these flowers just as He made roses and lilies, and I think He likes them just as much."

Anyone arranging flowers in a church should do so in a spirit of reverence and humility, for it is a privilege to be able to contribute to a service for the worship and glorification of God. Self-pride should be forgotten, and only the fact considered that, like music, what the arranger does with flowers helps create a setting to lift the spirits of the entire congregation.

I remember when I went early one Easter morning to check the arrangement I had done the day before. The organist and soloist were rehearsing for the morning service. I stood alone in the sanctuary, surrounded by the sweet fragrance of lilies, with warm spring sunlight streaming across the altar, listening to the glorious strains of "I Know

That My Redeemer Liveth." The message of Easter was never more clear.

Be Organized

A committee, as suggested, is an ideal way for organizing the arrangement of church flowers. The privilege should be shared. If some members who are interested but less talented than others work with those more experienced, they will soon feel more confident. Also, a committee is a group that can talk about matters relating to church flowers with the officials of the church. Expenses for new containers or mechanical supplies can be discussed with the budget committee. In one church where the choice of material was restricted because the minister wanted the altar flowers to be taken to sick people in the parish after the service, the flower committee was able to explain that because the stems of flowers were cut in different lengths for altar arrangements, they could not always be assembled successfully in another container. And that by using material such as foliage and wildflowers which looked attractive in the church, but was not suitable for taking to the sick, money otherwise spent to buy flowers could be used for a fund to provide flowers for the sick and shut-ins.

Knowing Your Church

Some churches have established rules about what may or may not be placed on the altar and other parts of the church. If this is so, the rules must be followed, but otherwise there is great latitude. In thinking of flowers for the church, the first thing to consider is the architecture of the building. This will govern the type of arrangement. It is easy to understand that although a mass arrangement would be equally appropriate in either a massive Gothic church or a classic Colonial one, the first would be larger and more impressive and the second would be simpler and more restrained.

Then there are other things to be considered. Does the church have a chancel, or is the pulpit on a platform behind the Communion table? This would affect the placement. Are the windows stained or clear glass? This affects the light. Is there a dorsal hanging on the wall behind the altar? This would affect the color. Is the cross on the altar, or does it hang above it? This would affect the size of the arrangements.

The altar appointments usually consist of a cross, candlesticks, and altar vases. The latter are often handsome tall brass vases with narrow-necked openings. (Ways to use these will be described later.) Instead of always using the same altar vases, a flower committee might use some of its budgeted money to buy others as a permanent investment. There are many inexpensive ceramic vases of good design and classic shape that make excellent church vases. Low brass planters relate well to brass candlesticks. Pottery vases can be painted a color that blends with the other appointments and repainted for variation. For very large churches, tall pedestals to hold large arrangements are effective when placed at the sides of the altar.

The Arrangements

Two things to especially keep in mind in making an arrangement in a church are *size* and *color*. If the cross is on the altar, the arrangements should never be taller than the cross. Of course, if it is hanging behind the altar, the arrangements can be in proportion to the space this governs. Also, an arrangement that seems large to you as you are making it will look much smaller from the rear of the church. Therefore, as you are working, it is a good idea to walk to the rear to make sure that the arrangement doesn't look diminished.

Also keep in mind colors that tend to recede—blue, purple, lavender, blue-green, and green-blue. You may have done a beautiful arrangement with blue iris at the focal point, but from the rear of the church it will look as though there is a hole in the middle. I have seen arrangements for weddings of white flowers with blue ones added to match the bridesmaids' dresses. Unfortunately, only the bridal party at the altar is conscious of the blue accent.

Also, it is important to consider stained glass. Sometimes, if such windows are prominent, you can take a color cue from them. However, if a stained-glass window is directly in back of the altar, its dominance should be considered. I was in a church recently where such was the case, and from where I was sitting I could barely distinguish the outline of the cross against the window, let alone the flowers. In this instance it would have been a better choice to do the altar vases with dark green foliage and use flowers in pedestal arrangements on either side of the chancel steps.

Liturgical churches use different-colored frontal altar cloths for different festivals and periods of the church year, and those who arrange the flowers should be aware of these when planning their arrangements. In churches where there are pillars in the aisles, for times such as Easter or Christmas or for weddings, you can enclose Oasis in cages of chicken wire and fasten them high on the pillars. By putting flowers in the Oasis from the top, sides, and bottom, you get a stunning bouquet and they are high enough to be effective.

Flowers for churches should have fairly bold forms and good lasting qualities. Dainty flowers are beautiful at close range, but their effectiveness is lost at a distance. Different foliage used alone, or with an accent of flowers, is attractive. What could be more beautiful in a small country church with white pews and red carpeting than autumn leaves in glorious colors?

Since it is best to do the flowers in place, always have drop cloths to cover the altar and floor below so that drops of water won't stain the wood, or so that bits of plant material won't get ground into the carpet. It is best to do the arrangements the day before as many churches have early services. If you spray your arrangements and cover them with plastic, they will keep fresh; although, since most church buildings are cool, it often isn't necessary.

Since each church is different, perhaps the easiest way to discuss different kinds of arrangements is to tell about the ones in the church with which I am most familiar. The suggestions can then be adapted to other churches:

This particular church is a small Episcopal one at the seashore. The interior is of paneled wood with narrow stained-glass windows. Behind the altar is a dorsal of deep red, and hanging in front of the dorsal is a huge wooden cross. The chancel rail, the candlesticks, and altar vases are of handsome brass.

The altar vases are of a typical shape with narrow necks. They are not always used, but when they are, if a piece of Oasis is wedged in the neck so that two or three inches extend above the mouth of the vase, you can make a much larger arrangement than if all the stems had to go into the narrow neck, because you can put some into the sides of the Oasis. If you want the arrangement to be larger and taller still, you can use one of the cones on a spike (see the section on Mechanical Aids) or you can tape a large pill bottle to a piece of very heavy wire (the wire will take less room in the neck of the container than a heavy stick).

These vases are not always used for mass bouquets. Sometimes there is a line arrangement on each side of the altar, starting high on the outside and curving low toward the foot of the cross. The low curve is made possible by sticking the stems up into the Oasis.

One of the members of the congregation has a particularly beautiful piece of driftwood. This is very suitable with the wooden cross and is sometimes used in place of vases. Its silhouette, curving from high on one side of the cross, underneath it, to a point on the other side, is decorative in itself, but is breathtaking when the flower heads of pink and red mallows (which live for a day out of water) are placed along the main line.

Another favorite way of treating the altar is to put a brass planter filled with Oasis at the foot of the cross. Tall, curved branches which seem to be embracing the cross are placed at either end of the planter, and the latter is filled with flowers, perhaps daisies, or pink geraniums (the color pink which complements the red dorsal), or pale yellow day lilies which relate to the brass. The day-lily heads are fastened to florists' picks. The flowers are arranged low in the planter across the foot of the cross and follow partway up the curving branches. At Christmas this treatment was beautiful with branches of English holly, and instead of the planter, pots of pink and white poinsettias, especially chosen for size and uniformity, were placed on their sides across the bottom so that one looked directly into the flowers.

On a Sunday when *Communion* is being celebrated, the arrangements may be of wheat and grapes to symbolize the bread and wine. Glass bowls, which fit into the top of the candlesticks, are filled with Oasis and line arrangements made with sprays of wheat forming the top line, and grapes curving to make the lower. With these, additional candlesticks are used at a lower level.

An innovative design, related to a seashore church, was displayed on the Sunday that stunning pieces of branch coral were used on either side of a huge fluted clamshell filled with wild seashore material— brown cattails, goldenrod, reed grass, and Queen Anne's lace.

High above the dorsal in the gabled roof of the church are two stained-glass windows featuring lilies. At Easter, they seem to cry for duplication in the tall altar vases.

At Easter and Christmas, it is the custom in many churches to decorate with plants so that they can be taken to invalids and shut-ins after the service. If this is so in your church, try to get plants of matching sizes graduating from large to small. Then you can mass them for a lovely effect. Nothing looks more spotty than individual pots placed here and there. Be sure that the pots are not covered with foil, which attracts the light and detracts from the plants. Instead, hide· the pots with foliage.

These plants are prettiest when they are tilted so that you look directly into the flowers. Sometimes you can rent the kind of stands from a florist that permit them to be tilted forward, but if you don't have these, just placing the pots on their sides works very well.

These are but a few of the many fascinating ways to work with flowers in churches. There are many books devoted to this subject alone. It is rewarding to read them and learn more about the symbolism of the different crosses, biblical objects and their symbols, flowers of the Bible, the major events of the church year, and the liturgical colors used with them. From all of these you will get inspiration.

Community Activities

To a person who has learned to cope with the mechanics, flower arranging can be tranquilizing and self-absorbing.

However, it is not a selfish art. A flower arranger can be of great value to her community, her church, and her fellow man. I love the cartoons about flighty portly ladies and their "tra-la-la" approach to flower arranging—in fact, I collect them. But most of the ladies I know don't fit the picture. They work too hard to be portly, and their approach is common sense, and often dollars and cents.

It is common for a flower arranger to hear a voice at the other end of the telephone say, "Will you do the flowers for the church supper (or the PTA tea, or the Community Chest dinner, or the Scout Father and Son Banquet)? The voice invariably adds, "Of course, we don't have much money to spend."

There you have the problem. As anyone knows who has ever done it, it takes a lot of material to make arrangements for several long tables. Also, to be effective, the containers should be similar. If the request comes when there is outdoor material, it isn't as difficult. Some members of the committee may have garden flowers, and there is always the roadside and field material. There is still the problem of containers, however.

At one church supper the problem was solved this way. There were plenty of marigolds available. The small amount of money allotted went to buy two dozen metal bread pans (a permanent investment). These were painted brown. Instead of using Oasis, the pans were filled with crumpled chicken wire to hold the flowers. When the arrangements, in yellow, brown, and orange, were in place on the long tables, the effect was very festive. After the supper, the pans were stored, and used again at Christmas—sprayed gold and filled with greens and gold-painted pinecones.

In the autumn, among the prettiest and most inexpensive arrangements for long tables are pumpkins hollowed out and filled with autumn leaves.

I bless the day that I discovered candle boards—nothing more than pieces of board with holes drilled in them to hold candles. These can be made to hold as many candles as you wish. They can be stained or painted any color. You can either use the same size candles, or have them graduated from a tall one in the middle. Placed at intervals along a table, with greens or autumn leaves on the table between them, they are very gay.

It is amazing how, with a little thought, you can solve the problem of "no money." A group of citizens in a seashore town gave a luncheon to honor a well-loved official who was retiring. Less money spent on table decorations meant more money for a gift, so the committee was asked to "dream up something inexpensive." For a luncheon of three hundred, the table decorations cost exactly nothing.

Everyone at the shore collects driftwood, so the committee combed the town and borrowed pretty silvery-gray pieces which they spaced down the middle of the table. On the driftwood, they arranged flat heads of red, white, and pink mallows, the lovely flower of the hibiscus family that grows wild at the shore. Since the club where the luncheon was held was able to supply pink cloths, the whole effect was really charming.

At the Yacht Club, to which we belong, there is an activity that brings pleasure to many people. It is a very large club, and to make it gracious and welcoming, there is a committee of ninety women, who like to arrange flowers (three women a week for thirty weeks) and who "do" the flowers on the entrance table, the mantel, piano and coffee tables in the main lounge, and the ladies room. The nice part is that, although there is a budget for flowers, very little of it is used, as the arrangers try to be original with field and roadside material, unusual containers (like anchors, shells, ships' wheels, lanterns, and other nautical objects), as well as containers of their own like usabatas, epergnes, unusual baskets, and so on. The result is that other members who are nonarrangers are becoming interested, and it is not unusual to hear someone say, "I can't wait to see what the girls have done this week."

In a town, there are many places where a lovely arrangement brings pleasure to many people—a library, a hospital, a museum, or the foyer of a YMCA building.

A bright arrangement on a librarian's desk gives the same air of warmth and graciousness to the room that it does in your own house, and think how many people can enjoy it during a day. A beautiful arrangement in the lobby of a hospital can do much for the morale of the often troubled and apprehensive people who see it. This was proved by the unsolicited and anonymous letter received recently by a garden club. The woman who wrote it was thanking the club (which routinely provided arrangements for the hospital lobby). This one was a particularly lovely spring arrangement. The writer of the letter said that she had been very despondent, but that the beautiful arrangement with its message of beginning life gave her hope. She ended by saying that, to her, one such arrangement was worth more than many flower shows.

There are groups of women organized to provide bedside flowers for patients in veterans' hospitals. On certain days of the week people bring flowers to a central point. The women's group transports them to the hospitals and makes the arrangements. At Christmas and Easter they also trim the chapels and dining rooms.

In a town that has a fine museum, committees of women have done study and research to provide arrangements that are authentic in period for strategic places. The arrangements not only contribute to the beauty of the museum but are another aspect of its instruction.

I have already mentioned that I acquired one of my favorite containers at an antique show held as a fund raiser for the church. Dealers pay for space and give a commission on sales. Some of us who are interested in flower arranging make arrangements in the different booths. The dealers feel that this helps their sales and accounts for the long waiting list for this particular show.

These are but a few of the ways a flower arranger can contribute her talent to the community. There is almost no facet of community life where flower arranging hasn't a place.

Weddings

Weddings are lucrative and legitimate business for florists, and for those who can afford their flowers and services, there is no doubt that leaving the wedding decorations to them is an expedient solution. However, the expenses for a large wedding are so tremendous these days that many parents find themselves involved with estimates and charges for unexpected items to the point where pleasure in the wedding is counteracted by worry over the bills.

To these people "a flower arranging friend" willing to help is a godsend. And as for the friend, what great joy it is to contribute to the happiest occasion of a young couple's life. I know that this is true because I have done it many times, and any help that it has been to the bride or her family cannot measure up to the joy that I have had myself.

For a very large church wedding, the amateur would be wise to confine her efforts to arrangements for the altar, with well-placed palms or ferns rented from a florist as a background. (Altar arrangements are described in the section on Church Flowers. But for the small church or home wedding, there are many ways to make the surroundings beautiful and individual. For one thing, once it is known that a friend is "doing" the flowers for a wedding, other friends and neighbors may offer flowers from their yards and gardens, and you can take advantage of seasonal material like apple blossoms, rambler roses, lilacs, mock orange, white hydrangeas, and dogwood, which are a change from the usual carnations, snapdragons, gladiolus, and chrysanthemums.

I know of one elderly woman who grows unusually large and beautiful lilies of the valley by the thousands. The week her granddaughter was to be married, they were in full bloom. She invited a dozen or so of her young friends to a "morning coffee picking party." The younger women picked the flowers in bunches of fifty, while the older woman fed them delicious homemade coffee cake and coffee. Some of the blossoms were taken to the florist to be made into the bride's bouquet, and the rest the grandmother made into miniature bride's bouquets (using the Oasis holders described in Part I under "Mechanical Aids") for the centers of the individual tables at the reception.

There is another woman, in a small Vermont town, who grows flowers in her garden primarily for the Sunday services in the little white church there, and for the wedding of any girl who is married there.

In a small church there are many ways to use flowers and greens to make it festive for a wedding. One that I had great joy in doing was a May wedding in a small Episcopal church at the seashore. It is a simple church, with varnished wooden walls and pews, a high vaulted ceiling, and a lovely filigree-brass chancel rail. The light is filtered through narrow stained-glass windows.

Instead of ferns or palms at the front of the church, we decided to use small natural seashore pine trees. A morning that I will always remember is the one when the bride's mother and I went into the spring woods to cut them. It had been raining, and the smell of the wet pine and moist spring earth mingled with the fresh smell of the sea was indescribable. We cut trees of various sizes, their new tips like pale green candles, piled them in a station wagon, and took them to the church, where we banked them on either side of the altar, using heavy wire fastened to inconspicuous nails to hold them in place. The wedding was to be on Saturday, and we did this on the Wednesday before.

On Thursday we decorated the center aisle. We fastened standards, made by nailing a rectangular piece of plywood to a wooden pole, at every fifth pew. These were just a little taller than the end of the pew, and were varnished the same color as the wood in the church. We secured them with broad elastic bands. We fastened an aluminum freezer pan, sprayed dark green, to the plywood top with Stickum, fitted a soaked block of Oasis in it, and put a little water in the pan to keep the Oasis wet.

In this, we made perky bouquets of well-hardened white marguerites, green clusters of pachysandra and huckleberry. We covered the elastic bands with a loop of white ribbon, tying the ends in a bow on the aisle side. The effect was of an aisle of daisy clusters. (These looked as fresh when we dismantled them several days later, as they did then.) In the altar vases we made large arrangements of white lilacs and more marguerites. The whole effect was one of elegant simplicity. A plus that we didn't plan was the fragrance of the pine in the church the day of the wedding. It was so fresh that you could actually see people sniffing as they entered the church.

Another time the daughter of the minister of a little church in New England was to be married. Days before the wedding, women of the church gathered greens from the surrounding woods and made yards of roping. The day before the wedding they fastened this in garlands around the inside of the church. They also made bouquets of garden flowers and put them in water to harden. A couple of hours before the ceremony, they tied the bouquets to the ends of the pews with white ribbon. Again, I have never forgotten the fragrance as I entered that church or the exquisite simplicity of the decorations. Best of all, many people had a feeling of sharing in the ceremony.

When one of my friends, a widow, was to be married again in a chapel, she bought pots and pots of beautiful white chrysanthemums. Some of us arranged these, against a background of ferns, into a garden on the platform in front of the pulpit. There, surrounded by intimate friends, the couple was married. After the ceremony, each friend was given a pot of chrysanthemums as a remembrance.

The most peaceful time I had in the fun but hectic days preceding the wedding of one of my daughters was the quiet hour I spent in the church the morning of the wedding arranging the altar flowers. Although the main decorations were done by a florist, I reserved for myself that sentimental treat. There was more sentiment involved than just arranging them, too, for my mother had grown the flowers, handsome white Canterbury bells, from seed. At the ceremony the flower bells, swaying in the gentle breeze from an open window, seemed to be making a contribution to the music of the service.

Sometimes a flower arranging friend cannot take on the responsibility of the entire decorations of a church but would like to share her talent and garden flowers in some way. Arrangements of flowers on tables in the narthex or foyer of a church, or outside the front doors, are gracious and welcoming. I am thinking of a white-painted Colonial church where tall green garden urns, filled with white peonies, flanked the opened outside doors. The flowers were grown by a neighbor of the bride and arranged by her. At another wedding, also in a white New England church, a friend cut seven-foot sprays of gorgeous crimson ramblers and arranged them in bronze umbrella stands at either side of the entrance.

Reception Tables

A great help to a bride's mother would be for a flower-arranging friend to be responsible for the bouquets on the small tables at a reception. These should be done in similar containers, and ones easy to use for such an occasion are the metal Oasis holders. These are inexpensive and readily available. However, at two weddings I made good use of coffee cans. These were painted white, then dabbled with silver. Crumpled chicken wire made the mechanics.

At the first wedding, on a typical June day, the tables were covered with pink cloths and the cans filled with crimson rambler roses, which just matched the velvet seats on the caterer's chairs. At the other wedding, on a hot July evening, when the bridesmaids wore pale green and carried bouquets of glossy dark green leaves centered with gardenias, the tables had pale green cloths. I made bouquets of mixed greens— laurel, andromeda, ilex, and yew—in the white containers, and put a tall white candle in the middle of each. They looked cool and different.

If you are doing tables for a reception, and only white tablecloths are available, get ribbon in whatever color is being used for the bridesmaids' dresses and cross it over the white cloths. Make arrangements of white flowers in Oasis holders and place them in the center of the table where the crossed ribbons meet.

Sometimes a flower-arranging contribution can be as small as a nosegay for the top of a wedding cake. I know one woman who, learning that the tall stately bride was to carry calla lilies, made a miniature of her bouquet for the top of the wedding cake, using blossoms from her spathiphyllum house plant, whose flowers look like miniature calla lilies.

Index

Index

L

M